First World War
and Army of Occupation
War Diary
France, Belgium and Germany

29 DIVISION
Divisional Troops
Machine Gun Corps
29 Battalion
1 February 1918 - 31 October 1919

WO95/2294/3

The Naval & Military Press Ltd
www.nmarchive.com
Published in association with The National Archives

Published by

The Naval & Military Press Ltd

Unit 10 Ridgewood Industrial Park,

Uckfield, East Sussex,

TN22 5QE England

Tel: +44 (0) 1825 749494

www.naval-military-press.com

www.nmarchive.com

This diary has been reprinted in facsimile from the original. Any imperfections are inevitably reproduced and the quality may fall short of modern type and cartographic standards.

© **Crown Copyright**
Images reproduced by permission of The National Archives, London, England, 2015.

Contents

Document type	Place/Title	Date From	Date To
Heading	WO95/2294 29 Div 29 Bn Machine Gun Corps Feb 1918-Oct 1919		
Heading	29 Div Troops 29 Bn Machine Gun Corps 1918 Feb-1919 Oct To Independent Division Rhine Army		
Heading	War Diary Of 29th Battalion Machine Gun Corps From 1st Feby 1918 14th Feby 1918		
War Diary		01/02/1918	14/02/1918
Heading	War Diary Of "D" Coy. 29th Divisional M.G.Bth From 1.2.18 To 14.2.18		
War Diary	Line North Of Ypres	01/02/1918	12/02/1918
War Diary	Steenvoorde	13/02/1918	14/02/1918
Heading	War Diary Of 86th Machine Gun Company For February 1918 Volume 20		
War Diary	Brandhoek	01/02/1918	05/02/1918
War Diary	Dead End Ypres	06/02/1918	13/02/1918
War Diary	Steen Voorde	14/02/1918	14/02/1918
Heading	War Diary Of The 87th Machine Gun Company (Volume XXI) From 1st Feb 1918 To 14th Feb 1918		
War Diary	Dead End Ypres	01/02/1918	05/02/1918
War Diary	Front Line	05/02/1918	13/02/1918
Heading	War Diary Of 29th Bn Machine Gun Corps From 14-2-18 To 28-2-18 (Volume I)		
War Diary	Steenvoorde	15/02/1918	28/02/1918
Heading	War Diary Of 29th Battalion Machine Gun Corps. From 1st March 1918, To 31st March 1918. (Volume 11)		
War Diary	Steenvoorde	01/03/1918	07/03/1918
War Diary	Line	08/03/1918	31/03/1918
Heading	29th Divisional Troops. 29th Battalion Machine Gun Corps April 1918		
Heading	War Diary Of 29th Bn. Machine Gun Corps. From 1-4-18 To 30-4-18. (Volume III)		
War Diary	Goudberg Sector	01/04/1918	08/04/1918
War Diary	St. Jan Ter Biezen	09/04/1918	09/04/1918
War Diary	Neuf Berquin	10/04/1918	10/04/1918
War Diary	N. Berquin	10/04/1918	10/04/1918
War Diary	Neighbourhood Of N. Berquin	10/04/1918	12/04/1918
War Diary	Vieux Berquin	12/04/1918	12/04/1918
War Diary	Neighbourhood F.V. Berquin	13/04/1918	13/04/1918
War Diary	N. Of Vieux Berquin	14/04/1918	14/04/1918
War Diary	St Sylvester Cappel	15/04/1918	15/04/1918
War Diary	St Jan Ter Biezen	10/04/1918	10/04/1918
War Diary	La Creche	11/04/1918	13/04/1918
War Diary	Ravelsberg	14/04/1918	15/04/1918
War Diary	La Creche	13/04/1918	13/04/1918
War Diary	In Neuve Eglise	14/04/1918	20/04/1918
War Diary	St Sylvestre Cappel	16/04/1918	17/04/1918
War Diary	Hondeghem	20/04/1918	27/04/1918
War Diary	Line Meppe Forest	27/04/1918	30/04/1918
Heading	War Diary Of 29th Battalion. Machine. Gun. Corps. From 1st May To 31st May 1918 (Volume IV)		

War Diary	La Motte Sector (Right Division of XV Corps Front)	01/05/1918	05/05/1918
War Diary	La Motte Sector	05/05/1918	27/05/1918
Heading	War Diary Of 29th Battalion M.G. Corps. From June 1st 1918, To June 30th 1918. (Volume V)		
War Diary	La Motte Sector V Corps Front	01/06/1918	22/06/1918
War Diary	Blaringhem	23/06/1918	29/06/1918
Heading	War Diary Of The 29th Bn. Machine Gun Corps From July 1st To July 31st (Volume VI)		
War Diary	Blaringhem	01/07/1918	22/07/1918
War Diary	Croix Rouge	23/07/1918	23/07/1918
War Diary	Cassel	25/07/1918	26/07/1918
War Diary	Bavinchove Area	26/07/1918	31/07/1918
Heading	War Diary Of 29th Bn Machine Gun Corps From August 1st. To August 31st 18 (Volume VII)		
Miscellaneous	29th Division A	01/09/1918	01/09/1918
War Diary	Bavinchove Area	01/08/1918	03/08/1918
War Diary	Strazeele Sector Xv Corps Front	04/08/1918	31/08/1918
Heading	War Diary Of 29th Battalion M.G.Corps. From 1st Sept. To 30th Sept. 1918. (Volume VIII)		
Miscellaneous	29th Division "A"	13/10/1918	13/10/1918
War Diary	Bailleul Sector	01/09/1918	03/09/1918
War Diary	Between Bailleul And Armentieres	03/09/1918	05/09/1918
War Diary	W. of Bailleul	06/09/1918	10/09/1918
War Diary	Borre	12/09/1918	16/09/1918
War Diary	Proven	17/09/1918	21/09/1918
War Diary	St Jan-Ter-Biezen	25/09/1918	26/09/1918
War Diary	Vlamertinghe Area	27/09/1918	27/09/1918
War Diary	Zillebeke Lake Sector	28/09/1918	28/09/1918
War Diary	Gheluvelt	29/09/1918	30/09/1918
Heading	War Diary Of 29th Bn. Machine Gun Corps. From 1st Oct. To 31st Oct 1918. (Volume IX)		
War Diary	Line in Front of Gheluwe	01/10/1918	04/10/1918
War Diary	Pieeserue Area W. of Ypres	05/10/1918	05/10/1918
War Diary	Ypres Area	07/10/1918	10/10/1918
War Diary	Northen Rerens area IInd Corps	12/10/1918	12/10/1918
War Diary	Ledeghem Sector II Corps Front	13/10/1918	14/10/1918
War Diary	E Of Ledeghem	15/10/1918	15/10/1918
War Diary	Line N Of Heule	15/10/1918	17/10/1918
War Diary	Line W Bant Flys	17/10/1918	20/10/1918
War Diary	Line W. of St Louis	21/10/1918	24/10/1918
War Diary	Courtrai Area	29/10/1918	29/10/1918
War Diary	Marcq	30/10/1918	30/10/1918
Operation(al) Order(s)	29th Bn. M.G. Corps Order No. 31 Appendix B	06/10/1918	06/10/1918
Miscellaneous	29th Bn. M.G.Corps Appendix C	12/10/1918	12/10/1918
Operation(al) Order(s)	29th Bn. M.G.Corps Operation Order No. 35 Appendix F	14/10/1918	14/10/1918
Operation(al) Order(s)	29th Bn. M.G.Corps Operation Order No. 36 Appendix L	23/10/1918	23/10/1918
Operation(al) Order(s)	29th Bn. M.G.Corps Operation Order No. 37 Appendix N	26/10/1918	26/10/1918
Heading	War Diary November 1-30-1918. 29th Battn-Machine Gun Corps		
War Diary	Marcq Sh 36. K11a	01/11/1918	08/11/1918
War Diary	Luinghe	09/11/1918	09/11/1918
War Diary	St Sauveur. Sh 37/F21.a Celles (Sh37/D16) St Genois	10/11/1918	11/11/1918
War Diary	St Genois Sh 29/U16n	11/11/1918	11/11/1918

Type	Description	Date From	Date To
War Diary	St. Genois	12/11/1918	12/11/1918
War Diary	Celles Sh 37/Dn	13/11/1918	13/11/1918
War Diary	Flobecq. Sh 30/T27	14/11/1918	14/11/1918
War Diary	Lessines Sh38/C16	15/11/1918	15/11/1918
War Diary	Lessines	16/11/1918	17/11/1918
War Diary	Enghien Sh38/F26	18/11/1918	18/11/1918
War Diary	Enghien	19/11/1918	20/11/1918
War Diary	Braine-Le Chateau. (Brussels To 4.D.)	21/11/1918	22/11/1918
War Diary	Ohain (Brussels To 4.F.)	23/11/1918	24/11/1918
War Diary	Ceroux Mousty (Sh Brussels 6) 5.G.	25/11/1918	25/11/1918
War Diary	Corbais. (Sh Brussels 6) 5H	26/11/1918	26/11/1918
War Diary	Longchamps (Sh Brussels 6) 6K	27/11/1918	27/11/1918
War Diary	Antheit (Sh Liege 7) 6C	28/11/1918	28/11/1918
War Diary	Fraiture (Sh Marche 9 I.F)	29/11/1918	29/11/1918
War Diary	Remouchamps (Sh Marche 9 1.I)	30/11/1918	30/11/1918
Operation(al) Order(s)	29th Division Order No. 288 Appendix I	06/11/1918	06/11/1918
Miscellaneous	March Table		
Operation(al) Order(s)	88th Infantry Brigade Order No. 221	07/11/1918	07/11/1918
Miscellaneous	29th Division Operations Instruction No. 1	08/11/1918	08/11/1918
Operation(al) Order(s)	88th Infantry Brigade Order No. 222 Appendix 4	06/11/1918	06/11/1918
Miscellaneous	C Form. Messages And Signals		
Miscellaneous	Appendix 6		
Miscellaneous	C Form Messages And Signals		
Miscellaneous	Messages And Signals		
Miscellaneous	C Form. Messages And Signals Appendix 7		
Miscellaneous	C Form. Messages And Signals		
Miscellaneous	29th Division No. C.G.S 67/172 Warning Order Appendix 8	12/11/1918	12/11/1918
Operation(al) Order(s)	29th Division Order No. 291	13/11/1918	13/11/1918
Miscellaneous	March Table		
Miscellaneous	C Form. Messages And Signals Appendix 9	15/11/1918	15/11/1918
Operation(al) Order(s)	29th Bn. M.G. Corps Order No. 42		
Miscellaneous	29th Bn, M.G. Corps Order No. 42		
Miscellaneous	O.C.B Coy 29th Bn M.G. Corps	14/11/1918	14/11/1918
Miscellaneous	O.C.D Coy 29th Bn M.G. Corps	15/11/1918	15/11/1918
Operation(al) Order(s)	29th Division Order No. 290	13/11/1918	13/11/1918
Operation(al) Order(s)	29th Division Order No. 293 Appendix 10	16/11/1918	16/11/1918
Operation(al) Order(s)	29th Bn M.G. Corps Order No. 41		
Operation(al) Order(s)	29th Bn. Machine Gun Corps Operation Order No. 40	13/11/1918	13/11/1918
Operation(al) Order(s)	29th Bn. M.G. Corps. Operation Order No. 43 Appendix 11	17/11/1918	17/11/1918
Operation(al) Order(s)	Appendix "A" To 29th Division Order No. 293		
Miscellaneous	March Table (To Accompany 29th Div. Order No. 293)		
Operation(al) Order(s)	88th Infantry Brigade Order No. 230 Appendix 12	20/11/1918	20/11/1918
Operation(al) Order(s)	29th Battn. M.G. Corps. Operation Order No. 45 Appendix 13	22/11/1918	22/11/1918
Operation(al) Order(s)	29th Battn. M.G. Corps. Operation Order No. 44	20/11/1918	20/11/1918
Miscellaneous	March Table Issued With 88th Infantry Brigade Order No. 230	26/11/1918	26/11/1918
Operation(al) Order(s)	88th Infantry Brigade Order No. 232 Appendix 14	24/11/1918	24/11/1918
Miscellaneous	March Table Issued With 88th Infantry Brigade Order No. 232	24/11/1918	24/11/1918
Miscellaneous	March Table To Accompany 88th Infantry Brigade Order No. 231	22/11/1918	22/11/1918
Operation(al) Order(s)	88th Infantry Brigade Order No. 231	22/11/1918	22/11/1918
Operation(al) Order(s)	88th Infantry Brigade Order No. 233 Appendix 15	25/11/1918	25/11/1918

Miscellaneous	March Table To Accompany 88th Infantry Brigade Order No. 233 Of 25th Novr., 1918	25/11/1918	25/11/1918
Miscellaneous	29th Bn. M.G.Corps	25/11/1918	25/11/1918
Operation(al) Order(s)	86th Infantry Brigade Order No. 297 Appendix 16	25/11/1918	25/11/1918
Miscellaneous	29th Battalion Machine Gun Corps. Move Orders For 26th November 1918	25/11/1918	25/11/1918
Miscellaneous	88 Bde No. B4/290	25/11/1918	25/11/1918
Miscellaneous	Messages And Signals		
Miscellaneous	29th Battalion Machine Gun Corps	27/11/1918	27/11/1918
Miscellaneous	A Form Messages And Signals Appendix 17		
Miscellaneous	Messages And Signals		
Miscellaneous	29th Bn. M.G. Corps Move Orders For Nov 28th 1918	27/11/1918	27/11/1918
Heading	29 Bn M G Corps Vol 10		
Heading	D.A.G. G.H.Q. 3rd Echelon		
Heading	War Diary 1st-31st Dec. 1918 29th Bn. Machine Gun Corps Vol 11		
War Diary	Remouchamps (Sheet Marche 9) 1.I	01/12/1918	03/12/1918
War Diary	Francorchamps (Sheet Marche 9) 1.L	04/12/1918	04/12/1918
War Diary	Weismes Sh I.M.	05/12/1918	05/12/1918
War Diary	Montjoie (Sh LL. Ref 1 LG)	06/12/1918	06/12/1918
War Diary	Niddeggan (Sh LL. Ref 8.J)	07/12/1918	07/12/1918
War Diary	Erp (Sh IL Ref 6N)	08/12/1918	08/12/1918
War Diary	Sulz (Sh 2L. Ref 2B)	09/12/1918	12/12/1918
War Diary	Berg Gladbach (Sh. 2L Ref 1.E)	13/12/1918	20/12/1918
War Diary	Stumpe & Debringhausen. (Sh 2K-Ref 10.F)	21/12/1918	26/12/1918
War Diary	Stumpe & Debringhausen	27/12/1918	31/12/1918
Miscellaneous	March Table For Dec 1 Appendix I		
Miscellaneous	March Table For Dec 2		
Miscellaneous	A Form Messages And Signals		
Miscellaneous	36th Inf. Brigade 65/58	02/12/1918	02/12/1918
Miscellaneous	I M. East Hr		
Operation(al) Order(s)	86th Infantry Brigade Order No. 298	03/12/1918	03/12/1918
Miscellaneous	March Table-Issued In Conjunction With Brigade Order 298		
Miscellaneous	Messages And Signals Appendix 2		
Miscellaneous	A Form Messages And Signals		
Miscellaneous	Signals		
Miscellaneous	29th Div. No. C.G.S. 65/205	06/12/1918	06/12/1918
Miscellaneous	A Form Messages And Signals Appendix 3		
Miscellaneous			
Miscellaneous	Messages And Signals		
Miscellaneous	March Table For Dec 7 Appendix 4		
Miscellaneous	A Form Messages And Signals		
Miscellaneous	Appendix 5 Messages And Signals		
Miscellaneous	A Form Messages And Signals		
Miscellaneous	A Form Messages And Signals Appendix 6		
Miscellaneous	Messages And Signals		
Miscellaneous	Messages And Signals Appendix 7		
Miscellaneous	Messages And Signals		
Operation(al) Order(s)	29th Division Operation Order No. 310 Appendix 8	19/12/1918	19/12/1918
Miscellaneous	March Table. (To Accompany 29th Div. Order No. 310)		
Miscellaneous	29th Bn. M.G. Corps. Operation Order No. 47	20/12/1918	20/12/1918
Miscellaneous	2/Ht A.F Gusly		
Miscellaneous	C Form. Messages And Signals		

Heading	Rhine Army Southern Division Late 29th Division 29th Btn Machine Gun Corps Jan-Oct 1919		
Heading	War Diary. 29th Battalion Machine Gun Corps. 1st-31st January 1919 Vol 12		
War Diary	Dabringhausen & Stumpe Sheet 59 Coln	01/01/1919	31/01/1919
Miscellaneous	O.C. "A" Coy 29th Bn. M.G. Corps. No. 5 Labour Cory. Q.M. 29th Bn. M.G. Corps Appendix I	03/01/1919	03/01/1919
Miscellaneous	C Form Messages And Signals	02/01/1919	02/01/1919
Heading	War Diary. 29th Battn Machine Gun Corps 1st To 28th February. 1919 Vol 13		
War Diary	Stumpf & Dabringhausen Sheet 2K F10	01/02/1919	18/02/1919
War Diary	Stumpf & Dabringhausen Sheet 2K Germany F. 10	19/02/1919	28/02/1919
War Diary	Stumpf Dabringhausen & Grunewald	01/05/1919	31/05/1919
War Diary	Stumpf & Dabringhausen	01/06/1919	15/07/1919
War Diary	Stumpf & Dabringhausen	01/07/1919	31/07/1919
War Diary	Stumpf & Dabringhausen	16/07/1919	30/08/1919
War Diary	Stumpf, Germany	01/09/1919	30/09/1919
War Diary	Stumpf Nr Cologne	01/10/1919	31/10/1919

WO95/2294
2a DIV
2a Bn Machine Gun Corps   Feb 1918 - Oct 1919

29 DIV TROOPS

29 Bn Machine Gun Corps

1918 FEB — 1919 OCT

TO INDEPENDENT DIVISION
RHINE ARMY

Confidential.

War Diary
of
29th. Battalion. Machine Gun Corps.

From 2s.

1st July 1918.   14th July 1918.

Army Form C. 2118.

original copy

WAR DIARY
or
INTELLIGENCE SUMMARY.
(Erase heading not required.)

89TH COMPANY, MACHINE GUN CORPS.

Date: 1 - 2 - 18

Place	Date	Hour	Summary of Events and Information	Remarks and references to Appendices
	1/2/18		An inspection relief took place in the evening, Nos 2 & 4 sections relieving Nos 1 & 3 sections in the forward positions.	
	3/2/18		Relief on an average of two men per team went up to the line. Work detailed by the A.D.O.C. Division was undertaken by our teams from the various gun teams.	
	5/2/18		The Coy was relieved in the line according to Div. Order, at WIELTJE the teams returned to the Lgt Rly and were conveyed to BRANDHOEK to billets. Coy the remainder of the Coy of other ranks had their early in the day. A hot meal was ready for the troops coming out of the line. 2nd/Lt R BARR, Cpl SHARMAN & Hon. CAMPBELL proceeded on a A.A. gun course at LEWIS AERODROME.	
	4/2/18 7/2/18		The forenoon was occupied by cleaning all guns & getting the machine Lewis gun ammunition replenished for all while Coy in the forward area. Teams were in anticipation of transport by use of O.C. Brigade Col C. Roe Kitts to be heard _____ from HQ London. Fayette Sub day 1918, T. E. Yeoman 2/Lt & A.W. Legge M.C. to be but not having deceased, RSM 2/4C, Lt NICHOLS have arrived to together with a forward post as per program.	
	8/2/18			

Army Form C. 2118.

WAR DIARY
or
INTELLIGENCE SUMMARY.
(Erase heading not required.)

Instructions regarding War Diaries and Intelligence Summaries are contained in F. S. Regs., Part II. and the Staff Manual respectively. Title pages will be prepared in manuscript.

Place	Date	Hour	Summary of Events and Information	Remarks and references to Appendices
	9/2/18		The Coy was inspected by the G.O.C. Brigade. A message from Brigade notified the following award to personnel of this Coy the Belgian Croix de Guerre, Conspicuous Gallantry Companies.	
			BELGIAN CROIX DE GUERRE No. 31977 SGT. T. BIRNER D.C.M.	
	10/2/18		As per programme.	
	11/2/18		The Coy moved to STEENVOORDE by rail, the transport proceeding by road. 2/Lt J.W. DREVSON, Lt E.L. EVANS proceeded with the troops to make arrangements for billetting of all ranks prior to the arrival of hot meal was ready for the troops when they arrived in camp.	
	12/2/18		As per programme. 2/Lt R.F. GASDEN "Goolded", and PTE B.F. Payne No. 11032 PTE BAILEY proceeded on a Coy Cooks Course. No. 11381 PTE MERRE proceeded on a Sanitary Course.	
	13/2/18		As per programme. The C.O. attended a lecture by G.O.C. Division of which all C.Os were present	
	14/2/18		As per programme. The D.M.G.C. and were present at proball the C.O. & 2nd M. G. Coys in the Division were to inspect.	

J.J. Pailim CAPTAIN,
COMMANDING 88TH COY. M.G.C.

Army Form C. 2118.

WAR DIARY
or
INTELLIGENCE SUMMARY.

(Erase heading not required.)

CONFIDENTIAL

WAR DIARY

OF

"D" Coy.

29th DIVISIONAL M.G.B.

From 1/1/18 to 1/4/18

Army Form C. 2118.

WAR DIARY
or
INTELLIGENCE SUMMARY.
(Erase heading not required.)

Instructions regarding War Diaries and Intelligence Summaries are contained in F. S. Regs., Part II. and the Staff Manual respectively. Title pages will be prepared in manuscript.

Place	Date	Hour	Summary of Events and Information	Remarks and references to Appendices
June North of Ypres	1.2.18		Four Emergency Gun emplacements started at WURST FARM. Situation normal. Strength Officers 11 Strength O.R. 172.	
	2.2.18		O.C. returned to Coy. H.Q. at KOREK.	
"	3.2.18		Officers at Gallipoli reconnoitred with view to sending up the eight guns & gun teams from WIELTJE. Advanced Coy. H.Q. moved to GALLIPOLI	
"	4.2.18		Gun teams & eight guns moved up from WIELTJE to GALLIPOLI. 2/Lt Jones evacuated to U.K. Strength Officers 10 Strength O.R. 172.	
"	5.2.18		Gun teams at KOREK and WURST Fm. relieved by teams from GALLIPOLI. One O.R. evacuated. Strength Officers 10 Strength O.R. 171.	

Army Form C. 2118.

WAR DIARY
or
INTELLIGENCE SUMMARY.

(Erase heading not required.)

Instructions regarding War Diaries and Intelligence Summaries are contained in F. S. Regs., Part II. and the Staff Manual respectively. Title pages will be prepared in manuscript.

Place	Date	Hour	Summary of Events and Information	Remarks and references to Appendices
Line North of Ypres	6.2.18		Emergency positions at WURST FM completed. One O.R. sent on Course to U.K. Strength Officers 10 Strength O.R. 170	
"	7.2.18		Transport moved from DEAD END to Coy. Rear H.Q. at WIELTJE	
"	8.2.18		Gun teams at WURST FM and KOREK relieved. Five O.Rs transferred from 88th M.G. Coy. Strength Officers 10 Strength O.R. 175	
"	9.2.18		Situation normal.	
"	10.2.18		Situation normal. One O.R. evacuated sick to U.K. Strength Officers 10 Strength O.R. 174	
"	11.2.18		Orders for Coy. relief received.	

Army Form C. 2118.

WAR DIARY
or
INTELLIGENCE SUMMARY.
(Erase heading not required.)

Place	Date	Hour	Summary of Events and Information	Remarks and references to Appendices
June North of YPRES	12.2.16		Coy relieved by B Coy of 6th Div. M.G. Bn. Mn. Transport moved via POPERINGHE to STEENVOORDE. Relief completed by 5.0 p.m. Personnel moved to STEENVOORDE by lorry	
STEENVOORDE	13.2.16		Training. Strength Officers 10. Strength O.R. 174	
		10.2.16 9-12.0 Training 2 pm-3 Baths	Strength Officers 10. Strength O.R.174	

G. Hudson.
Capt.
O.C. "D" Coy. 29th Div. M.G.Bn.

War Diary

of

86th Machine Gun Company

for

February 1918.

Volume 20.

Army Form C. 2118.

WAR DIARY
or
INTELLIGENCE SUMMARY.
(Erase heading not required.)

Instructions regarding War Diaries and Intelligence Summaries are contained in F. S. Regs., Part II. and the Staff Manual respectively. Title pages will be prepared in manuscript.

Place	Date 1918	Hour	Summary of Events and Information	Remarks and references to Appendices
BRANDHOEK	February 1–4			
	5th		The Company paraded daily at 9 a.m. & carried out the programme of work laid down.	
"			During the afternoon the Company proceeded by march route to the Support Area & encamped at DEAD END YPRES.	
DEAD END YPRES	6th		The morning was spent in improving the camp. In the evening the Company supplied a carrying party to the forward area.	
"	7th 8th		These days were spent in improving the camp.	
"	9th		In the early morning 10 guns of the Company moved into the line to relieve 8 guns of the 89th M.G. Coy & 2 guns of the 150th M.G. Coy. The remainder of the Company with 4 guns moved into the line.	
	10th		Holding the line.	
	11th 12th			
	13th		On the afternoon of the 12th the transport moved to STEENVOORDE. The Company was relieved in the line by guns of the 5th Division & were conveyed by buses to the camp of 29th Divl M.G. Battalion at STEENVOORDE.	
STEENVOORDE	14th		The Company came under the administration of the 29th Divl M.G. Battn & became A Coy of that Battalion	

CONFIDENTIAL.

WAR DIARY.

OF THE

87th Machine Gun Company

(VOLUME XXI)

From 1st Feb. 1918 to 14th Feb. 1918.

Army Form C. 2118.

WAR DIARY
or
INTELLIGENCE SUMMARY.
(Erase heading not required.)

Place	Date	Hour	Summary of Events and Information	Remarks and references to Appendices
DEAD END YPRES.	1st		3.O.R. Taken on strength of Company from Base.	
	5th		Company proceeded to Front Line (Passchendaele Sector) and relieved the 88th Machine Gun Company. All 16 guns were in the line, 8 in front line system, 8 in support. Gun positions were as follows:—	
			Nos 1 & 2 Guns – D.6.a.9.5 } No 2 Section	
			Nos 3 & 4 " V.30.c.5.3 }	
			Nos 5 & 6 " V.30.c.1.9 } No 4 Section	
			No 7 Gun V.29.d.2.6 }	
			No 8 Gun V.29.c.9.7 }	
			Nos 9 & 10 Guns D.5.c.8.3 } No 1 Section	
			Nos 11 & 12 " D.5.d.2.2 }	
			Nos 13 & 14 " D.4.b.2.2 } No 3 Section	
			Nos 15 & 16 " D.3.b.9.9 }	
			Company H.Q at D.10.b.5.5	
			All guns were given barrage targets on which to fire in case of S.O.S, and direct lines in case of an enemy breakthrough.	

WAR DIARY or INTELLIGENCE SUMMARY

Army Form C. 2118.

Place	Date	Hour	Summary of Events and Information	Remarks and references to Appendices
France		5th	1.O.R. Taken on Strength of Company from Hospital.	
"		7th	4 O.R. Transferred to 87th M.G. Coy: from 88th Coy.	
		10th	Sector was changed from "B" to "A" in consequence. at 4.30 a.m. Nos 1,2,3,4,5,6,7 & 8 guns were relieved by 86th M.G. Coy. No 2 Section proceeded to CANAL BANK, in support & 4 mens positions were taken up by No 1 Section in left Sector as follow:— 2 guns — V.29.c.7.8. & 2 guns D.4.a.8.6. Company H.Q. moved to D.4.a.9.3. 1.O.R. Wounded (accidentally) 1.O.R. Returned from Hospital	
		13th	At 3.30 a.m Company was relieved by a Company of 8th Div: M.G. Battn with the exception of 2 positions at V.29.c.7.8 which were evacuated. On relief the Company (Less Transport which moved on 12th inst:) proceeded by Motor Lorry to STEENVOORDE.	

J. Michener
Capt.
Commdg. B. Company
29th Div. M.G. Battalion

CONFIDENTIAL

WAR DIARY
of
29th Bn. Machine Gun Corps.

(VOLUME I.)

From 14-2-18

To 28-2-18

WAR DIARY or INTELLIGENCE SUMMARY

Army Form C. 2118.

Place	Date	Hour	Summary of Events and Information	Remarks and references to Appendices
STEENVOORDE	15.2.18		The four Machine Gun Companies of the Division were amalgamated to form the 29th Battalion Machine Gun Corps.	
do.	15.2.18 to 28.2.18		This period was spent in the organising and training of this newly formed Battalion. Companies practiced their own in it formed of M.G. work and in handling of guns. All Companies spent some time on M.C. firing on ranges near CASSEL. Large drafts of men from the Infantry Battalions were posted into Classes under specially selected NCO's to be trained in Machine gunnery. The Battalion took part in Infantry Bde. ceremonial parades. The last 3 days of the month were spent in preparing for a ceremonial Parade as a Battalion. The strength of the Battn. on 28.2.18 was 42 officers and 707 O.R.	

[Signed] Lieut. Col.
Cmdg.
29th Bn. M.G. Corps

CONFIDENTIAL.

Vol. 2

WAR DIARY of

29th BATTALION MACHINE GUN CORPS.

FROM 1ST MARCH 1918, TO 31ST MARCH 1918.

(VOLUME 11)

Army Form C. 2118.

WAR DIARY
INTELLIGENCE SUMMARY.
(Erase heading not required.)

Instructions regarding War Diaries and Intelligence Summaries are contained in F. S. Regs., Part II. and the Staff Manual respectively. Title pages will be prepared in manuscript.

Place	Date	Hour	Summary of Events and Information	Remarks and references to Appendices
STEENVOORDE	1.3.18		Practice for Ceremonial Parade inside Cadre Office.	
"	2.3.18		Ceremonial Parade and Inspection by Major General Sir A. B. de Lisle Commanding the Division. Battalion marched past in two columns form.	
"	3.3.18		About Church Parade. Last draft of men from Reserve Battalion joined the Battalion.	
"	4 - 6		Training and preparation to go into the Line.	
"	3.3.18			
"	7.3.18 2.0 p.m.		Battalion marched to GODEWAERSVELDE and entrained for YPRES arriving there at 3.30 pm. Transport went by road & arriving at YPRES. A.B.C and D Coys. marched to IRISH FARM Camp WIELTJE while B's HQ went to the HQ camp DEAD END YPRES. Transport were at DEAD END	
LIME	8.3.18		The Battalion relieved the 8th Battalion M.G. Corps in the GOODBERG sector N of PASSCHENDAELE.	
			C Coy relieved 16. Rifle Bde. with HQ at LIMKEEK D Coy the Lt Lester with HQ was Pill Box 63. B Coy in reserve to support Co	

WAR DIARY
INTELLIGENCE SUMMARY.
(Erase heading not required.)

Army Form C. 2118.

Place	Date	Hour	Summary of Events and Information	Remarks and references to Appendices
"	6.3.18		w/e. HQ at GALLIPOLI. A Co. remained in Reserve in DEAD END.	
LINE	11.3.18		The enemy raided the Division on the right of VAT COTTAGES N. of PASSCHENDAELE. The 2nd Sub-Brigaders were in its front line but had to fall back on reserve. The fire f the Battalion did good work in assisting its repulse. Firing about 30,000 rds. SOS lines the Battalion in the line were not afterwards hit by front line troops. Wire Cutting which is followed took place. A Co. relieved C Co. in Right Sector. C Co. going to Support line at GALLIPOLI. B Co. relieved D Co. in Sector. D Co. going to DEAD END in Reserve.	
"	16.3.18		Whole Company relief. C Co. relieved A Co. in R. Sector. D Co. relieved B Co. in L. Sector. A Co. went to Support line and B Co. to DEAD END in Reserve.	
"	21.3.18		to form fully Battalion fired a Barrage for 20 mins. to cover the 332. Division on our R. in a raid on the GASOMETERS in front of PASSCHENDAELE. Village itself. Nearly 20,000 rds. were fired. The raid had small results, no accompanying troops but one enemy dead was afterwards reported.	

Army Form C. 2118.

WAR DIARY
or
INTELLIGENCE SUMMARY.
(Erase heading not required.)

Instructions regarding War Diaries and Intelligence Summaries are contained in F. S. Regs., Part II. and the Staff Manual respectively. Title pages will be prepared in manuscript.

Place	Date	Hour	Summary of Events and Information	Remarks and references to Appendices
Line	26.3.16		Relief of companies as follows. A Co. relieved C Co. in Right Section C.G. going to Dead End in reserve. B Co. relieved D Co. in Left Section D Co. going to Support line.	
"	31.3.16		Total casualties from 16 March to 31 March (inclusive) 5 Killed 25 Wounded.	

[signature] Lt Col. Cmdg.
2/5 B: W.G. Regt

29th Divisional Troops.

29th BATTALION

MACHINE GUN CORPS

APRIL 1918.

Vol 3

CONFIDENTIAL.

WAR DIARY
OF
29TH Bn. MACHINE GUN CORPS.

(VOLUME III.)

FROM 1-4-18. TO 30-4-18.

WAR DIARY
INTELLIGENCE SUMMARY
(Erase heading not required.)

Army Form C. 2118.

Place	Date	Hour	Summary of Events and Information	Remarks and references to Appendices
GOUDBERG SECTOR	1.4.18 onwards		The division was in the line in GOUDBERG SECTOR N. of PASSCHENDAELE	
"	3.4.18		C.C. Relieved A Co in the right sector and A Co relieved D Co in Support. D Co. took over the front line from the 33rd Bn. M.G. Corps on one night, were to reinforcement in the Corps area. B Co. remained in the L. Section.	
"	7.4.18		D Co. were relieved from the new R. Sector by the 415th Bn. M.G. Corps. 15 guns during descent to DEAD ENDS (M.15) night from Kimmer morning.	
"	8.4.18		Bn. moved by rail from ST. JEAN Siding to POPERINGHE marching from there to ST. JAN TER BIEZEN (Road Camp at F.25 d 6.0). C Co. was relieved in R. Echelon by the 415 Bn. M.G. Corps at or near half to when A Co. in Support. A Co. on relief moved to ST JAN TER BIEZEN by rail and road.	
[from the front the Battalion was divided into two parts. A separate diary follows for each.]				

WAR DIARY
INTELLIGENCE SUMMARY.
(Erase heading not required.)

Army Form C. 2118.

Place	Date	Hour	Summary of Events and Information	Remarks and references to Appendices
ST. JAN TER BIEZEN	9.4.18	10.30 a.m.	A and D Coys. Arrived Coys. A and D Coys. under the Command of MAJOR W.T. RAIKES M.C. (the Remainder of command) marched three times into 86th and 87th Infantry Bdes. leaving Biezen via the BOESINGHE — PROVEN road at about 9.0 a.m. from Kit bags and Sir Batt Boxes therefrom were carried in his remainder of this by following motor transport.	
NEUF BERQUIN	10.4.18	6.30 a.m.	A and D Coys. detrained at NEUF BERQUIN about 6.30 a.m. and moved Right about LISLE and a (Shorts 36 and 35a) One Platoon of 87th Bde. marched to support of the 50th Division which was fighting in ESTAIRES. and one section of D Co. occupied positions in support of them about L 28. The remainder of the Mjs. took up reserve positions in L 19 and L 30. the transport were in E 23 a. During the day an Enemy aeroplane was brought down by Lewis Gun fire by 87th Bde. its occupants captured. During the afternoon orders were received for the 86th and 87th Bdes. to move out at 5.0 p.m. to support the L. flank of the 51st Division which its Summary is	

WAR DIARY
INTELLIGENCE SUMMARY

Army Form C. 2118.

Place	Date	Hour	Summary of Events and Information	Remarks and references to Appendices
N. BERQUIN	10.4.18	6.0 p	bombard. The Bn's Bde. were to be relieved in the right sector, occupying in turn afternoon along the two streams from the bridge at SAILLY-SUR-LA-LYS in G.16 to LE PETIT MORTIER in G.14. 85th Bde were to be relieved to the left Bn. In the evening shortly afterward across the stream at STEENWERCK. D.Co. two 1 Lewis moved into Bn's. Bde; and A+ Co with 86th Bde to L.10.d.	
			At about 5.15 from Bn's to D.Co were having lft from Bde HQ in NEUF BERQUIN at L.10.a.10 a shell from a H.V. fm fell right in the middle of the lorry killing two officers and wounding two others, and causing casualties to 37 O.R. in Sh.Bn. then MAJOR G. HUDSON the adjt. D.Co. having reorganised the wounded was able to move it w.t 87th Bde at 5.45 p.m.	
			Before the 87th Bde had reached their new line, it was dark, and as the enemy had steady turned to Lys. The general line of the road from TROU BAYARD (G.15.c) NE to G.14 and G.9 was taken up. The further form were put in front the to straighten the line, the remaining return	

Army Form C. 2118.

WAR DIARY
INTELLIGENCE SUMMARY.
(Erase heading not required.)

Place	Date	Hour	Summary of Events and Information	Remarks and references to Appendices
Neighbourhood of N. BERQUIN	10.4.18	—	A & D Coys were in reserve.	
"	11.4.18	—	During the morning the enemy got round the left flank of the Division and Battalions of the 86th Bde. with 3 sections of A Co. were moved at 5.15 across to fill the gap so formed. The reserve sections of A and D Cos took up positions in a sunken RUE MONTIGNY in LIS.	
"	from		By midday ESTAIRES had been temporarily captured and the enemy advanced to the ESTAIRES – MERVILLE BERQUIN road. The 50th Division retiring to the RUE MONTIGNY – LILLE line. Our machine guns fired from Stephens three into the 86th Bde. in L17 and L18 had splendid targets and did great execution. Successfully covering the withdrawal of the infantry. Unfortunately 2 guns of A Co. under 2nd Lt JAMIESON became isolated and were later seen in action against the enemy who had practically surrounded them. In spite of this that element of the 50th Division was rallied and from were putting up a fine fight in a forward trench. At this time Lce Transport Sergt of D Co.	

WAR DIARY
INTELLIGENCE SUMMARY

(Erase heading not required.)

Army Form C. 2118.

Instructions regarding War Diaries and Intelligence Summaries are contained in F. S. Regs., Part II. and the Staff Manual respectively. Title pages will be prepared in manuscript.

Place	Date	Hour	Summary of Events and Information	Remarks and references to Appendices
Neuflandt PN. BERTHEN	11.4.18		SERGT. S. HESELTINE — did very fine work in keeping up his Lewis close to the front's repellers of stutikas. All Lewises were for away Snipers.	
"	12.4.18	2.30 am	At about 2.30 am the Boches with their tanks overran to a his many slung the road L7a 3.7 — L3c3.9 — L3c7.3 — the centre with the 86th Bde on the left and 89th Bde on the right. This had we already stiffened by 16 Manchus front of the 31st Division.	
		9.0 am	The enemy followed up this withdrawal very rapidly and by 9.0 am roughly he followed, adding Barrage, before our various parts of the new position, especially about the main road in L7a and across this own bomb was forced back. At his same time our Left Flank was turned round BOULIEU (in L5b). The Bns. were fought with the greatest determination and spirit throughout this day. Owing to this pressure on the L Flank it was decided to make a further withdrawal and to hold a line from the road junction in K6b through F15 central to BLEU in F20 a. During the fighting around BLEU after the infantry had fallen back the Mgs. went forward on their own and succeeded	

Army Form C. 2118.

WARDIARY
INTELLIGENCE SUMMARY.
(Erase heading not required.)

Instructions regarding War Diaries and Intelligence Summaries are contained in F. S. Regs., Part II. and the Staff Manual respectively. Title pages will be prepared in manuscript.

Place	Date	Hour	Summary of Events and Information	Remarks and references to Appendices
VIEUX BERQUIN	13.4.18	After noon	Began in billetting had the attack forward houses. During the afternoon the enemy captured OUTTERSTEENE and MERRIS. Still pushing Capuroy with L[ewis] guns. The infantry withdrew to the area. In action we found that the wire with the MG's of the 29th Br. 6 men p[er] Co. 3rd Br. M.G. Corps had been Boes were fired at from the trenches. Although the trenches had suffered considerably in the fighting, the few men [left] able to do fine work on the ground. The fire from F.A. Co. Public 1862S Sgt H. ORVIS did fine work by keeping his Lewis guns running as he tried to defend from the village.	
September L.V. BERQUIN	B.G. Evening		Began to harass the 2 from with 1862S Sgt H. ORVIS in 71 2d inflicted very heavy casualties with his Lewis gun behind a wood in Etc. The fire on the railway in F.7 do held up a [enemy?] attack developing S. of MERRIS. About midday the enemy captured VIEUX BERQUIN completely.	

WAR DIARY
INTELLIGENCE SUMMARY

Army Form C. 2118.

Place	Date	Hour	Summary of Events and Information	Remarks and references to Appendices
N. of NEUF BERQUIN	14.4.18	2.0	The remaining few teams of A and D Cos. were withdrawn during the night to 1st Australian Division which had come up into the line. Regrouped at ST. SYLVESTRE – CAPPEL	
St. SYLVESTRE – CAPPEL	15.4.18		The remainder of A and D Cos. were reorganised into 1 Co. of 16 from which were placed in reserve at the disposal of the 1st Australian Division	

WAR DIARY
or
INTELLIGENCE SUMMARY.
(Erase heading not required.)

Army Form C. 2118.

Place	Date	Hour	Summary of Events and Information	Remarks and references to Appendices
MT. ST JAN	10.4.19	1.0 p.m.	Band C Coys. and Battn. HQ.	
TER BIEZEN			Band C Coys. and Battn. HQ moved by lorries with 86th Infantry Bde. leaving a point on the POPERINGHE — ROUEN road at 3.0 p.m. to They detrained at L.20 p.m. at S.28.b.6.4 on the BAILLEUL — ARMENTIÈRES road from tripode & Boche men carried out the lorries, the many having driven in the trenches holding the report line E and S.E. of ARMENTIÈRES to Pte. Bde. and Rfts of B and C Coy. took up a line running from the W. edge of NIEPPE with the main road through RABOT, thence SW to a point 800 yards S. of STEEN WERCK Station S. of LA CRECHE.	
LA CRECHE	11.4.18	3.0 a.m.	During the night of the 10/11th the enemy patrols penetrated LE VERU W. of TROIS ARBRES	
		2.0 p.m.	The enemy attacked from N. & N.E. direction on the front of the 25th Division (on the L. of 86th Bde.) and in front of the 86th Bde. front. the attack to main road at a point about 800 x W. of PAPOT and forced Son of the 1st R. Newfoundland Regt. to return W. along the road. Two Platoons of B Coy. were this included in B.S.d. did great execution his men, although cut off, most of the teams being either killed or wounded.	

A6945 Wt. W14422/M1160 350,000 12/16 D. D. & L. Forms/C./2118/14.

WAR DIARY
INTELLIGENCE SUMMARY

Army Form C. 2118.

Place	Date	Hour	Summary of Events and Information	Remarks and references to Appendices
LA CRÈCHE	11.4.18		attack having been made & some time from reserve from were sent up on the left and took up positions centre and in B & C to defend the L. Flank.	
			the enemy retired in front but started new our front. Shrapnel which killed the enemy in the same number heavy Mg. fire from LAMPERNISSE and Rue du Sac.	
			At 12. noon 4/1st day the line ran W. of LAMPERNISSE Kings Crossroads at PONT d'ACHELLE to STEENWERCK STATION. During the night we withdrew from STEENWERCK Stn. in order to straighten the line.	
LA CRÈCHE	12.4.18		Shrapnel fire of enemy advanced in a N. direction our line running E. and W. from STEENWERCK – CABARET de SAULE at A.16.a.80.50. Large bodies of enemy with transport were seen on the road moving N. from CABARET de SAULE – PONT du PIERRE or A.10 central. These were engaged by 6 guns of C Co. in the vicinity of STEENWERCK STATION. Heavy casualties were inflicted. Three hostile attacks developed between PONT de PIERRE and STEENWERCK	

WAR DIARY / INTELLIGENCE SUMMARY

Army Form C. 2118.

Place	Date	Hour	Summary of Events and Information	Remarks and references to Appendices
La CRÈCHE	13.6.18		STATION. They were relieved with the 15th 2nd Hampshire Regt. and 1/5th Leicestershire Regt., will Sutherland Lights 6 from F.C. Co.	
"	13.6.18	2.15 pm	During the afternoon the enemy attacked in a N. direction from the railway line in A.Li.S and to the infantry were driven back and the MGs withdrew to conform, occupying a line 700 – 1000 yards S. of BAILLEUL – ARMENTIÈRES road.	
			At the same time an attack was delivered against the 34th Division on L flank. These troops fell back in conformance and retired to the L flank of the 88th Bde which was forced to conform and took up a line through WETSTEEN CABARET at B.16.40.90.	
			The from x which was in front in contact with us in B.14 Gun front suffered to the infantry but many to the enemy to the retirement of the 36th Division. All of the two 1 MO and 3 men were lost most of them being killed including the MO in charge 2nd Lt 6735'S Sgt Winter.	
	3.0 pm		During the afternoon six guns (two of C Co and 3 of B. Co) were shot out to the	

A6945 Wt. W14422/M1160 350,000 12/16 D.D. & L. Forms/C/2118/14.

Army Form C. 2118.

WAR DIARY
or
INTELLIGENCE SUMMARY.
(Erase heading not required.)

Place	Date	Hour	Summary of Events and Information	Remarks and references to Appendices
Lt CREOHE	13.4.18	3.0 p.m.	Left PLOETS and took up positions on the high ground in front of Tje ... and Tize ... to cover the Bde ... Btn. falling back from the direction of NEUVE EGLISE which has been lost and whither Lgts. 25's Division who were holding broken and weak. [A ... front of their Bn ... to form ... followed.]	
"	Night 13/14/18		According to orders received the line was withdrawn to position in the high ground N. of the main road. The line ran at 11.0 p.m. 13th. Through high ground in S31c and S31d. S23a and B.18c and ... the 23 from this line in action were Staffs withdrawn to the line after crossing the crossroads. After infantry were put in positions, C Co. at the Ridges. B Co. on its left. A Co. on its approaches to the high ground. The remaining forms were in reserve with Co. HQ.	
RAVELSBERG	14.4.19		Very heavy bombardment heavily occupied line a few being blown up at POTIER FARM in S23d. During the night the enemy fired light M.G.'s through machines out the high ground but were rounded up by 2 pm teams of C. Co. who	

A6945 Wt. W1422/M1160 350,000. 12/16 D. D. & L. Forms/C./2118/14

Army Form C. 2118.

WAR DIARY
INTELLIGENCE SUMMARY.
(Erase heading not required.)

Place	Date	Hour	Summary of Events and Information	Remarks and references to Appendices
RAVELSBERG	14.6.18		Killed about a dozen of this enemy and Captured 16 men and a light gun.	
"	16.6.18		Bn and C Co were relieved at dawn by some of the 5y'th Bn MC Corps. Bn they moved with Bn HQ and Transport to ST SYLVESTRE – CAPPEL by road moving via BAILLEUL, BERTHEN, MONT DES CATS and BERKE.	

Army Form C. 2118.

WAR DIARY
or
INTELLIGENCE SUMMARY.
(Erase heading not required.)

Instructions regarding War Diaries and Intelligence Summaries are contained in F. S. Regs., Part II. and the Staff Manual respectively. Title pages will be prepared in manuscript.

Place	Date	Hour	Summary of Events and Information	Remarks and references to Appendices
			The 6 Detached from 71st B and C Cos.	
Le CRÈCHE	13.4.18	3.0 pm	About 3.0 pm selection of C Co made Lt EATON L/S M.C. and information of B Co took up positions at T.7.c.2.2. T.7.c.9.9 and S.18.b.9.8. in Support of the 25th Division. At 7pm the enemy shelled these areas very heavily and an attack developed. The 25th Division which was holding the ridge in T.8 and 14 near MERVE EGLISE fell back to their support line in T.7.d.	
nr. MERVE EGLISE	16.4.18		Early in the morning small parties of the enemy were seen on the road in T.13.c. and b. There were M.G.s and Lewis guns and M.G.s and disposed. The day was quiet until about 6 pm when the enemy again attacked but was held in great strength. This was opposed by our M.G.s and Lewis fire and the enemy advanced in small parties using every yard cover from hedges, commencing in the valley in T.13.c. and T.9.c. They were driven by artillery fire.	

Army Form C. 2118.

WAR DIARY
INTELLIGENCE SUMMARY.
(Erase heading not required.)

Instructions regarding War Diaries and Intelligence Summaries are contained in F. S. Regs., Part II. and the Staff Manual respectively. Title pages will be prepared in manuscript.

Place	Date	Hour	Summary of Events and Information	Remarks and references to Appendices
				XIV
In MOVE ELVUE	15.4.18	9.0 a.m.	About 9.0 a.m. another hostile attack began. The infantry in S.18.b. advanced and the MG's were ordered to come back to conform. Our wt before they had engaged some very good targets.	
"	16.4.18	5.0 a.m.	The line was with drawn later miles and we to up the MG's went into reserve at 4.30 b.	
		5.0 pm	At about 5.0 p.m. the Saxons during the MG's (of which there were now only 4 guns) took up positions on the slopes of MOUNT KEMMEL at N25C5.0	
"	17.4.18	7 pm	At about 7.0 p.m. two guns were ordered to detrain to the 146th Inf. Bde at M28C 7.5 leaving MG. Barrage as another gun had been destroyed by shellfire on the 16th	
"	18.4.18		The remaining 3 guns returned to 88th Bde at M20a 5.5	
"	20.4.18		The 3 guns with their mules from 88th Bde. and returned back to Batt. HQ at HONDEGHEM on the 21st April	

A6945 Wt. W14422/M1160 350,000 12/16 D. D. & L. Forms/C./2118/14.

Army Form C. 2118.

WAR DIARY
or
INTELLIGENCE SUMMARY
(Erase heading not required.)

Place	Date	Hour	Summary of Events and Information	Remarks and references to Appendices
St SYLVESTRE CAPPEL	16.4.18		Reorganisation of Ambulances. The strength of the Batt: was 27 Officers and 643 OR.	
			Casualties were as follows in the week 8-15th April	
			A Co. 6 Officers 65 OR	
			B Co. 4 " 33 "	
			C Co. 1 " 15 "	
			D Co. 8 " 107 "	
			A total of 19 Officers and 220 OR killed wounded & missing.	
"	17.4.18	3.0 p.m	The Composite Co. formed from A and D Cos under MAJOR JP ROBERTS MC moved to LE PEUPLIER to be in immediate reserve to 1st Australian Division which was then attacking with its flanks. It was not called upon to fight and remained in billets at LE PEUPLIER	
"	17-19.4.18		Work was carried out on the HAZEBROUCK defences for which units were sited and entrenchment were dug in the vicinity of BORRE, ROUGE CROIX, PRADELLES and PAPOTE.	

Army Form C. 2118.

WAR DIARY
or
INTELLIGENCE SUMMARY.
(Erase heading not required.)

Instructions regarding War Diaries and Intelligence Summaries are contained in F. S. Regs., Part II. and the Staff Manual respectively. Title pages will be prepared in manuscript.

Place	Date	Hour	Summary of Events and Information	Remarks and references to Appendices
HONDEGHEM	20.4.18	2.0 p.m.	HQ, B and C Coys moved to HONDEGHEM bynoud advance lined by A and D Coys from LE PEUPLIER back on the HAZEBROUCK defences was continued. The Battalion was unable to move by day and thus by night Reorganisation of Battalion completed and four Companies again formed.	
"	23.4.18		A and D Coys with then transport moved to billets at MORBECQUE bynoud for Bn. HQ. in order to be more conveniently placed in Cavalry reserve line should have to be occupied. The rest of the Bn. remained at HONDEGHEM	
"	27.4.18		The Battalion relieved the 3rd Bn. H.L. Centre in the line on the front E11A — K4C. The right sector of the IV Corps front. Companies took over the line as follows: A Co : Right forward B Co : Left Reserve C Co : Left forward D Co : Right Reserve	

Army Form C. 2118.

WAR DIARY
or
INTELLIGENCE SUMMARY.
(Erase heading not required.)

Place	Date	Hour	Summary of Events and Information	Remarks and references to Appendices
LINE: MOEPE BOESR.	27/4/18		Bn. HQ was in informs of D11 a.R.O Transfer lines and Bn. Svcs it D12.2.4	
"	28-30/4/18		The four positions which had previously been very badly shed and badly suffered, were entirely reorganised and sited. Huts were begun on the new emplacements. No water running four inislated points in the enemy lines were begun on the 30th instant.	

[signature] LIEUT.-COLONEL,
COMDG. 29th BN. M.G. CORPS.

CONFIDENTIAL

WAR DIARY

OF

29TH BATTALION · MACHINE · GUN · CORPS.

(VOLUME IV.)

FROM 1ST MAY to 31ST MAY 1918.

WAR DIARY or INTELLIGENCE SUMMARY

Army Form C. 2118.

Place	Date	Hour	Summary of Events and Information	Remarks and references to Appendices
LA MOTTE SECTOR (Ryn Divn) XXI CORPS Front)	1.5.18		No change of importance on the Divisional Front. Much harassing fire carried on by Artillery and M.G.'s on roads and tracks around VIEUX BERQUIN.	
"	Night 2/3		Heavy Gas shelling of Bois d'AVAL and roads round LA MOTTE.	
"	3.5.18		Inter Company relief: D Coy relieved A Coy in the Right forward area B Coy relieved C Coy in left forward Sector. Relief accomplished without incident	
"	4.5.18		Preparation for a raid carried out by the Bn. Sig'd defnsly Bde in the Left front sector.	
"	5.5.18		At 1.5 am E & F Border Regt raided in many places the objective was to raid in E11d from trench junction E11d 35.40 — E11d 30.75. 3 prisoners and a light M.G. were captured. The raiders lost in officers (killed) and 3 O.R. (wounded).	

A6945 Wt. W14422/M160 350,000 12/16 D. D. & L. Forms/C/2118/14

WAR DIARY or INTELLIGENCE SUMMARY

Army Form C. 2118.

Place	Date	Hour	Summary of Events and Information	Remarks and references to Appendices
LA MOTTE Sector	5.5.18		The trenches were inspected & and Cy. frons in MMs Glenth point out pulling down & protecting dumps in front of tres midiers.	
"	6.5.18		A raid was carried out by Nrs. 85th Infantry Brigade on BERDULIEU FARM in E.29.d. The 1st Lancashire Fusiliers raided at 2.50 am assisted by our artillery and M.G. fire. The result was unknown as the farm was found unoccupied though there were signs of recent work and wiring. We suffered no slight casualties.	
"	7.5.18 -8.5.18		During the night 7/8.5.18 at 2.0 am Gas projectors were fired upon E.29.c.5.5., E.29.d.3.8, and E.29.d.5.6.	
"	9.5.18		Inter-Co. relief. A and C Co. moving into the forward positions B and D coming back into "Suffolk".	
"	10.5.18		Heavy Gas shelling during night 10/11th on roads and in BOIS D'AVAL.	

WAR DIARY
or
INTELLIGENCE SUMMARY.

Army Form C. 2118.

Place	Date	Hour	Summary of Events and Information	Remarks and references to Appendices
LA MOTTE SECTOR	14.5.18		Battalion HQ. handed back to VIGC R.6 near WALLON CAPPEL.	
"	10-14 5.18		Inter training for turned out during the whole of this period. A few dud bombs were thrown during the E. edge of the BOIS d'AVAL in E.21.d and E.27.b.&.d. Smoke trench in the undergrowth running NE and SE and these were found fires were lit to fire down these clearings. Parrour patrols were made in house in LA MOTTE being reinforced by training and rifle "Battle" shooting made in.	
"	15.5.18		Divn. to relief carried out in wood & carried out without incident.	Mm
"	16/17 5.18		Discharge & Inspection by the Divisional front is about 1.30 am	Mm
"	21.5.18		A raid was carried out by the 6/8th Infantry Bde. At 11.26 pm shots of 2nd R WALES BORDERERS raid the enemy line at E.23.c 20.70 and E.23.c 20.99.3	Mm

Army Form C. 2118.

WAR DIARY
or
INTELLIGENCE SUMMARY.
(Erase heading not required.)

Place	Date	Hour	Summary of Events and Information	Remarks and references to Appendices
LAMOTTE SECUR	21.5.19		in the vicinity of Plug Farm. The artillery and MG's cooperated in the raid & this company captured one Light MG and three casualties were inflicted. The raiders lost 1 Officer (killed) and 3 OR (wounded).	
"	2.5.19 -27.5.19		A raid was carried out by 87th Infantry Brigade. Eight 1st K.O.S.B.'s against a MG's situated at E17 a 90.80 and E17 a 98.70. MG's cooperated in the raid. The raiders went over at 2.15 am. One of his MG's was captured while 3 men lay utter to have moved previously and were not clear from Barrage. The 1st K.O.S.B.'s had 3 OR wounded.	

Shuttleworth Major
for LIEUT.-COLONEL,
COMDG. 29th BN. M.G. CORPS.

Vol 5

CONFIDENTIAL

WAR DIARY

OF

29TH BATTALION M.G. CORPS.

(VOLUME V.)

FROM JUNE 1ST 1918, TO JUNE 30TH 1918.

Army Form C. 2118.

WAR DIARY
INTELLIGENCE SUMMARY
(Erase heading not required.)

Place	Date	Hour	Summary of Events and Information	Remarks and references to Appendices
LA MOTTE JOSOR XV CORPS Front	1.6.18	Ref. map 36 a. NE.	Preparations for Minor Operation to be carried out by 86th Brigade against LUG FARM and ANKLE FARM in E 23 and 17. Cooperation with 1st AUSTRALIAN Div. (on our Left) arranged.	
"	night 1/2		Intercompany reliefs — A and C Coys going forward. B and D Coys coming into support.	hm
"	3.6.18		86th Brigade attacked LUG FARM. Two howrers in E 23 a 80.60. ANKLE FARM up to E 17 c 60.50. The operation was a complete success. 31 prisoners and 9 light MGs being taken. A number of germans were killed. The trenches for B. Cooperated, 12 from being taken. Special tasks during the operation.	
"	night 3/4		Intercompany relief. B and D Coys going forward. A and C coming back to support.	hm

A6945 Wt. W14422/M1160 350,000 12/16 D. D. & L. Forms/C./2118/14.

Army Form C. 2118.

WAR DIARY
INTELLIGENCE SUMMARY.
(Erase heading not required.)

Place	Date	Hour	Summary of Events and Information	Remarks and references to Appendices
LAMOTTE ?? ?? to Corps Inv'n	13.6.18	—	Reorganization of Second Zone positions in accordance with Corps Instructions. Orders sent to Batteries concerning the manning of their alternative Positions. Orders issued with S.O.M.	—
"	night 13/13		Inter Company relief carried out: A and C Ers to Personnel lines, 'B and D' ones back to Staffer.	
"	14.6.18		Information received that an attack was imminent. Ammunition, water etc. inspected and Divisions warned to be vigilant.	—
"	15.6.18		In accordance with orders from Dgl Div: all Emplacements in Second Zone were manned by reserve from Batt's. had 5/6 guns in action.	
"	16.6.18		No hostile attack took place.	
"	night 16/17		Usual fire was brought over Enemy lines in E 24, 18 and 30.	—

WAR DIARY
INTELLIGENCE SUMMARY.
(Erase heading not required.)

Army Form C. 2118.

Place	Date	Hour	Summary of Events and Information	Remarks and references to Appendices
LAMOTTE SECTOR & CORPS RESERVE	18.6.18	—	4 forms received one Coy of 2nd LEINSTER REGT. in a Small operation near LUSP FARM. Small operations from ANGLE POST which had been retaken by the enemy on the 10th.	
"	night 19/20		Interior Company reliefs — B and D Coys going forward — A and E Coy coming back to Support.	
"	20.6.18		The Division was relieved by the 31st Division. D Coy of the MGR Bn. was relieved in Right forward Sector on night of 20.6.18 and went back to its Divisional Reserve Bn. Camp at D.B. a 9.9 for the night.	
	"		A, B and C Coys were relieved under Date 6.18. D Coy marched to Billets at BLARINGHEM. A and B Coys on relief went to Div. Reserve Bn. Camp, C Coy near to Camp at BEEK-HOUT-CASTEEL at C.5.d.70.95.	
	22.6.18		Bn. HQ A and B Coys marched to Billets at BLARINGHEM leaving C Coy at BEEK-HOUT-CASTEEL.	

Army Form C. 2118.

WAR DIARY
INTELLIGENCE SUMMARY.
(Erase heading not required.)

Place	Date	Hour	Summary of Events and Information	Remarks and references to Appendices
BLANGERMONT	23.6.18	—	The locations of the Battn. were as follows: HQ. at B.22.c.30.70, A Coy at B.22.c.30.25, B Coy at B.22.c.70.70, D Coy at B.22.d.70.15 (one C Coy remaining at C.15.d.70.95.)	
			The day spent in cleaning up.	
	24.6.18 – 28.6.18		Company training began. Training parades for Coy instructors and NCOs. Special parades in afternoon for Officers and NCOs. 30c range built for the Coys. Coys. Officers reconnoitre Army Battle line. Battalion studying orders and instructions in the event of attack. Positions allotted to Companies.	
	28.6.18		Coys. were up into Left Support positions to assist 31st Division in a total operation.	
	29.6.18		Parties for Lewis gun parade on Rifle Grenade in B3b by Companies. Parade with Limbers.	

[Signature] Lieut.-Colonel,
Comdg. 29th Bn. M.G. CORPS.

CONFIDENTIAL

WAR DIARY

of the

29th Bn. Machine Gun Corps

(VOLUME VI.)

From JULY 1ST to JULY 31ST

Army Form C. 2118.

WAR DIARY
INTELLIGENCE SUMMARY
(Erase heading not required.)

Instructions regarding War Diaries and Intelligence Summaries are contained in F. S. Regs. Part II. and the Staff Manual respectively. Title pages will be prepared in manuscript.

Place	Date	Hour	Summary of Events and Information	Remarks and references to Appendices
BLARINGHEM	1.7.18		Elementary Technical Training carried out in Billets. Practice for Ceremonial Parade.	
"	2.7.18	2.30 pm	The Battalion with fighting limbers was inspected by MAJOR GEN. DE. CAYLEY. C.in.C. Excdy: 29th Division. on the Polo Ground in B26.c. The Battalion marched past in column of companies, followed by its fighting limbers in columns from line.	hm
"	3.7.18		Company training in Billets, and ⅓ Special for parade under Divisional for Officer.	
		2.30 pm	Officers on Tactical Staff Ride under C. of. Officer.	
"	4-5 7.7.18		Company training and firing on 25" Range.	
"	6.7.18		D Coy were taken to long range at LUMBRES by lorry and carried out Part I firing at H.G. Course.	hm
"	6.7.18		Coys. relieved the Batt'n. from BECK-HOUT-CASTELL by march route.	hm

WAR DIARY / INTELLIGENCE SUMMARY

Army Form C. 2118.

Place	Date	Hour	Summary of Events and Information	Remarks and references to Appendices
BLARINGHEM	8.7.18	—	A and B Coys went to LUMBRES for Musketry Firing.	
"	9.7.18		General Divisional Holiday for Divisional Horse Show.	
"	10- 13.7.18		General Divisional & Brigade training in the field. Started in Divisional Area to the West of BLARINGHEM.	
"	13.7.18		B Coy under orders from the Corps C.R.S., went with its lines in its Rifles Batt. Sector of the STRAZEELE SECTOR, relieving an Australian M.G. Coy and coming under orders of OC 15th Australian M.G. Bn.	
"	16.7.18		D Coy and 2 Sections of A Coy went in lorries to LUMBRES to take part in a Brigade Tactical Scheme with 85th Inf Bde.	
"	17-20 7.18		Section Training in the Field and Tactical work under O.C. Coys in Training Area.	
"	18.7.18		A Coy and 2 Sections of D Coy took part in a Brigade Tactical Scheme to in BLARINGHEM area. 85th Inf Bde.	

Army Form C. 2118.

WAR DIARY
or
INTELLIGENCE SUMMARY.
(Erase heading not required.)

Place	Date	Hour	Summary of Events and Information	Remarks and references to Appendices
BLARINGHEM	25.7.18	9.0 a.m.	The Bn. paraded and marched to ROUGE CROIX N. of CASSEL under orders from 29th Division G.S. Route was via PONT ASQUIN – ERBLINGHEM – THIOD – MAISON BLANCHE – TROIS ROIS – ZUYTPEENE – L'ANGE – Bn. HQ established at I.35.c.60.50 (sheet 27)	
CROIX ROUGE – CASSEL	26.7.18		Technical training in Billets.	
"	27.7.18		B Coy rejoined Bn. from 1st Australian MG Bn. being relieved by a Company of 61st Bn. MG Corps.	
"	28.7.18		Under orders from 29th Div: Battalion marched to BAVINCHOVE area, marching via CASSEL and CASSEL Station. Bn. HQ established at O26.c.35.05	
BAVINCHOVE area	29.7.18		Section training in Battalion area. Officers Recce's and Nos 1 and 2 Special Sn. branches training in Brigade.	
"	30.7.18		Coys relieved a Company of 61st Bn. MG Corps in R. Buffs sector, STRAZEELE Sector coming under OZ R. Another s/s B.	

Ph... ...ng ? Lt Col.
COMDG. 29th BN. M.G. CORPS.

CONFIDENTIAL

WAR DIARY

OF

29TH Bn MACHINE GUN CORPS

FROM AUGUST 1ST. TO AUGUST 31ST 18.

(VOLUME VII)

29th Division G.A.

   Herewith original War Diary for the month of August, 1918.

                              Lieut.Colonel,
                         Comdg 29th Bn. M.G.Corps.

Q/591

1st September 1918.

WAR DIARY
INTELLIGENCE SUMMARY

Army Form C. 2118.

Instructions regarding War Diaries and Intelligence Summaries are contained in F. S. Regs., Part II. and the Staff Manual respectively. Title pages will be prepared in manuscript.

(Erase heading not required.)

Place	Date	Hour	Summary of Events and Information	Remarks and references to Appendices
BAVINCHOVE area	1.8.18		A Coy moved to STRAZEELE Sector & Coys front and relieved left forward Coy. 1st AUSTRALIAN M.G. Bn — Coming under Command of 1st Bn. O.C. 1st Battalion. H.Q. of A Coy was at W14.c.30.75 (Sheet 36.c)	
"	2.8.18		D Coy relieved 2nd Zone Coy of 1st Australian M.G. Bn in 2nd Zone of STRAZEELE SECTOR.	
"	3.8.18		B Coy relieved Reserve Coy of 1st AUSTRALIAN M.G. Bn into H.Q. at L'HOTTAND (V.23.c). Battn. Headquarters moved to V.22.a.8.2 where it relieved H.Q. of 1st Australian M.G. Bn. Command passed at midday.	
STRAZEELE Sector & Coys front	4 — 6 8.18		Both positions sited in Divisional lines and work started on them.	
"	7.8.18		Inter Company reliefs as follows:— D Coy relieved A Coy in Left Forward Sector; B Coy relieved C Coy in Right forward Sector; A Coy relieved B Coy in 2nd Zone positions; C Coy came back to reserve.	

A6945 Wt. W14422/M1160 350,000 12/16 D. D. & L. Forms/C. 2118/14.

Army Form C. 2118.

WAR DIARY
or
INTELLIGENCE SUMMARY.
(Erase heading not required.)

Place	Date	Hour	Summary of Events and Information	Remarks and references to Appendices
SPANBROEK Sector XV Corps Front	8-12 8.18		Work in trenches carried on. Re: inclement carried out. Elephant shelter put in and positions revetted and camouflaged.	
"	13.8.18		Intertraining starts. A Coy relieving D Coy in L. Forward Sector. B Coy in R. Forward Sector. B Coy relieving A Coy in Zone. D Coy coming back to rest.	
"	17.8.18		In view of our operation about to take place – Bttn moved to take Barrage positions at X25d 20.10 and 12 from & D Coy moved to same place.	hm
"	18.8.16		The divisional attack to Outersteene Ridge in conjunction with an attack on our left by 9th Division. (Zero hour 11.0 am) Advanced Bn HQ. W30 to 9.8. 28 guns in close fired a Barrage in support of the attack. 4 guns of A Coy were emplaced at F1 a 7.5 to support wired tanks. 4 guns under SSgt Russ of D Coy were formed into 69th Bde (1st KOSB) unit to assist tanks of taking TERRAPIN HOUSE. 4 guns under 2/Lt Burgess of A Coy moved forward with 2/Lt Burgess of A Coy. The operation was wholly successful. The HOEGENACKER SPUR was captured	hm

Army Form C. 2118.

WAR DIARY
– or –
INTELLIGENCE SUMMARY.
(Erase heading not required.)

Instructions regarding War Diaries and Intelligence Summaries are contained in F. S. Regs., Part II. and the Staff Manual respectively. Title pages will be prepared in manuscript.

Place	Date	Hour	Summary of Events and Information	Remarks and references to Appendices
GRAZIERE Sector of the Cojeul River	18.8.18		And out line established along the railway in F31655 – F31d00 – F3a0.1 – F26d8.5 – Runs along railing to ALBERT CROSSING. Casualties in the Bn: 1 Officer wounded. 1 OR & of friends. 8 wounded.	hm.
	19.8.18		Successful minor operation by 2LC? Sgt Bake assisted by 4 guns of the H.G. Bn. 4 guns of C Coy fired from E6a70.60: 4 guns of C Coy fired from E6d 80.50 4 guns of D Coy fired from X36c 68.55 to assist the attack. An outpost line being established in our new line from F6d 50.50 – along road running SW to F13a 70.20 – F13c 40.60	hm.
	20.8.18		Machine gun Defence rearranged. 46 new positions started and occupied by A B and C Coys. (D Coy in Reserve) Drawings and camouflages started.	hm.
	21.8.18		Inter Company reliefs: D Coy relieved A Coy in L. Fontaine Estre. Barrel Covys later Sections relief only.	
	23–28 8.18		Posts and outposts and entrenched. Enemy harassed by night with indirect fire	hm.

Army Form C. 2118.

WAR DIARY
INTELLIGENCE SUMMARY.
(Erase heading not required.)

Instructions regarding War Diaries and Intelligence Summaries are contained in F. S. Regs., Part II. and the Staff Manual respectively. Title pages will be prepared in manuscript.

Place	Date	Hour	Summary of Events and Information	Remarks and references to Appendices
STRAZEELE Section of the Corps Front	29.8.16 to 30.8.16	—	Enemy retirement which had for some time been forecasted, began on Div¹ front. Patrols of Bn's and Lgh Bdes with mobile Sections of Machine Guns followed enemy closely. At midday on 30ᵗʰ August our line was as follows:— BAILLEUL STATION — A 7b 00.60 — MOOTE BOOM — GAUL FARM.	✓
	31.8.16	—	Enemy retirement continued slowly followed by our patrols. A Bge moved forward with 89ᵗʰ Inf. Bde. Withdrawing their HQ at 5.26.2.5. At night fall the Divisional line ran approximately : PITCH FARM (S. of LA CRECHE) — A 16 central — LA BECQUE — ALA.2.	✓

A6945 Wt. W14422/M1160 350,000 12/16 D. D. & L. Forms/C./2118/14.

(CONFIDENTIAL) Vol 8

WAR DIARY

OF

29th Battalion M.G.Corps.

FROM 1st SEPT. to 30th SEPT. 1918.

(VOLUME VIII)

29th Division "A".

   Herewith WAR DIARY for the month of
September 1918.

R. 702

13th Oct. 1918.   [signature] Major,
                              Comdg 29th Bn. M.G.Corps.

WAR DIARY
INTELLIGENCE SUMMARY.

(Erase heading not required.)

Army Form C. 2118.

Instructions regarding War Diaries and Intelligence Summaries are contained in F. S. Regs., Part II. and the Staff Manual respectively. Title pages will be prepared in manuscript.

Place	Date	Hour	Summary of Events and Information	Remarks and references to Appendices
BAILLEUL SECTOR.	1.9.18		The Division continued its advance on its own without delay from position to position.	Ref. Sheets 27 and 36.
"	"	6.0 a.m	At 6.0 a.m. B Coy became attached to 88th Infantry Bde. and moved along to operate with left flank Divisional front with X Corps then HQ. was established at S.10.c 10.30. (N.E. of BAILLEUL). Our line now runs A.15.c. 0.2. — along road to A.10.c. Central — along light railway to A.6.c. 0.8 — S.29.6.2.9.	Summary of B Coys Operations See Schedule hereto
	2.9.18	—	Line moved forward to a line running N and S from BULFORD CAMP in S.28.c. 30.00. — Cross roads DE SEULE at B.31.d 10.90. Regtl HQ. moved to A.16.c. 60.10.	
	3.9.18		Advance continued. Bldg from were established in position on E side of NEUVE EGLISE — DE SEULE road between BULFORD CAMP and T.25 & 70.60. 1500 yards to the NE of BULFORD CAMP DE NIEPPE French systems were taken over by the Division at 7.10 a.m. and the	
		7.10 a.m		

WAR DIARY or INTELLIGENCE SUMMARY

Army Form C. 2118.

(Erase heading not required.)

Place	Date	Hour	Summary of Events and Information	Remarks and references to Appendices
# Bailleul	3.9.18	—	Line advanced in the neighbourhood of LES TROIS PIPES and NIEPPE.	
BAILLEUR and ARMENTIERES		11:0	The 86th Inf. Brigade with it attacked M.G. Company (D) moved this morning in yesterday W. of LA CRÈCHE. Dining this day 15. 26 of GHQ line (T2c central — T26a central) were occupied by the 86th Bde. Covered mostly by Sqns of B Coy.	
"	4.9.18		By night fairly Epr. on line rue B26 d — N. E. WATERLAND and TOUQUET PARMENTIER (incl.) — B17 central — B5 Central — E. of PLOEGSTEERT — "HYDE PARK CORNER" — trenches in W13 b and d — ROSSIGNOL FARM — IRASH FARM — STINKING FARM (U7a). 86th Bde in this advance assisted by the front of B Coy, captured HILL 63 in spite of great opposition and heavy shell fire. Bldgs suffered some 50 casualties in this attack. 100 prisoners were taken in the outskirts of the village of PLOEGSTEERT.	

A6945 Wt.W11422/M1160 350,000 12/16 D.D.& L. Forms/C./2118/14.

WAR DIARY or INTELLIGENCE SUMMARY

Army Form C. 2118.

Place	Date	Hour	Summary of Events and Information	Remarks and references to Appendices
Between BAILLEUL and ARMENTIERES	5.9.18	2.0 am	Our heavy trench mortars were made by the Enemy and the L. of the Battalion front near Hill 63. They were later repulsed with loss to the Enemy. (1 Officer 7 O.R. Captured).	
			The Division was relieved by the 31st Division. On the night 4/5th Companies moved out of the line & Bks and came to locations as under:-	
			A Coy X 24 c 3.4	
			B Coy X 21 b 2.0	
			C Coy X 29 b 3.6	
			D Coy X 28 d 6.3	
W. of BAILLEUL	6.9.18	-	General refitting and reorganisation. Coys informed. A and C Coys moved to X 29 c 90.90 and X 24 d 90.00 respectively.	
	10.9.18		Field training around BAILLEUL carried out.	
BORRE	13.9.18	-	Companies marched into BORRE — HAZEBROUCK area to be accommodated in farms and unoccupied houses on the HAZEBROUCK — BORRE road.	

WAR DIARY or INTELLIGENCE SUMMARY

Army Form C. 2118.

Place	Date	Hour	Summary of Events and Information	Remarks and references to Appendices
BORRE	13.9.18	—	Dispositions of Companies as follows:-	
			A Company V23d 70.20	
			B " V24d 55.45	
			C " V23d 85.20	
			D " V24c 70.45	
			Bn. Head Quarters remained at W25c S.E. (near BORRE) and Qm. stores moved to V23d 40.30.	
	13- 16.9.18		Training and refitting for fresh Operations. Companies were all billeted at LA KREULE.	
"	16.9.18		Division moved into II Corps Area. The Battalion moved at 11.0 am. personnel by train from HONDEGHEM (entraining – in tin trains) detraining at PROVEN. Transport marched by road at 8.0 am. Battalion went into Camp at PEKIN CAMP (F2c 10.60)	
PROVEN	17-21 9.18		Training round Camp. Companies all fired in Range near CROMBEKE.	

Army Form C. 2118.

WAR DIARY
or
INTELLIGENCE SUMMARY.
(Erase heading not required.)

Place	Date	Hour	Summary of Events and Information	Remarks and references to Appendices
PROVEN	19.9.16	—	Company relieved a Company of the 14th Bn M.G. Corps in the line in front of YPRES in the vicinity of ZILLEBEKE LAKE.	
"	21.9.16	—	Company was relieved by 3 Battalions of the 1st Motor Machine Gun Bde. which are attached to the Division.	
ST JAN-TER-BIEZEN	25.9.16	—	The Battalion travelled by road to ROAD CAMP, ST. JAN-TER-BIEZEN (F25c) arriving at 5.30 pm.	
"	26.9.16	—	A, B and D Coys and Quartermasters Stores moved to ORILLA CAMP (B26c 90.00) near VLAMERTINGHE at 7.0 am. Battn HQ. B began at 10% personal after stove companies moved to BRAKE CAMP. (A30c) at 7.30 pm.	
VLAMERTINGHE	27.9.16	—	At 6.0 pm A, C and D Companies came under Brigades to which they were attached — Hampson to 86th, Rea + C Coy to 88th Rea and Day to 87th Bde. B Coy remained in Reserve.	

WAR DIARY
or
INTELLIGENCE SUMMARY

Army Form C. 2118.

Place	Date	Hour	Summary of Events and Information	Remarks and references to Appendices
VLAMERTINGHE area	25.9.18	7.0 pm	A C and D Coys marched under Brigade orders to assembly positions close to YPRES-VLAMERTINGHE - main road E YPRES - road junction H.12.d.3.4. from were carried on pack animals entirely by C Coy and party on foot and partly by limber, eg A and D Coys. B Coy. and transport of HQ. and Rear Bn. HQ. moved E ORILLIA CAMP.	
ZILLEBEKE LAKE area	26.9.18	5.30 am	The Division took part in an attack with enemy positions E. of YPRES in which the Second Army and 2nd Belgian army on L. Operated. The 85th and 87th Btns attacked at Zero hour (5.30 am) with the M.G. Coys attached E then (A and D). After the capture of the CLAPHAM JUNCTION - STIRLING CASTLE ridge the 88th Brigade was to carry the attack to 26th and 87th Btns. In the afternoon B Coy moved up from ORILLIA CAMP and came under orders of GOC 86th Infy Bde.	

WAR DIARY / INTELLIGENCE SUMMARY

Army Form C. 2118.

Place	Date	Hour	Summary of Events and Information	Remarks and references to Appendices
GHELUVELT	30.9.18		The advance was continued about the Ypres – MENIN road. KRUISEECKE was then [strongly held] by the enemy.	
			30th September the Bn was brought to W. outskirts of GHELUVELT. There were Nine 2 Brigades in the line and the M.G. Coy was to support –	
			A Coy with 8th Bde on the high ground to the MW of GHELUWE. B and C Coy with 9th Bde round GHELUWE and on to KRUISEECKE ridge to W. of GHELUWE and D Coy with Sgt Bde near KRUISEECKE.	

(CONFIDENTIAL)

WAR DIARY

OF

29th Bn. MACHINE GUN CORPS.

(VOLUME IX.)

FROM 1st Oct. to 31st Oct 1918.

Army Form C. 2118.

WAR DIARY
or
INTELLIGENCE SUMMARY.
(Erase heading not required.)

Instructions regarding War Diaries and Intelligence Summaries are contained in F. S. Regs., Part II. and the Staff Manual respectively. Title pages will be prepared in manuscript.

Place	Date	Hour	Summary of Events and Information	Remarks and references to Appendices
Line in front of GHELUVE & GHELOWE	1.10.16	—	Bn of Mont 28, 29, 30 — PELIUM and TROMBE W. Bn. Divn. had men in front of GHELUVE (Q4) and though not Divn hqrs K34 at Bg. 88th Inf Bde with "C" Coy held outpost line of Division from in valley immediately W. of GHELUVE (Q3 and K34). 86th Inf Bn with "A" Coy, left high front in Suffort on left front — armed MOLENHOEK, high front (K27). 87th Inf Bde with "D" Coy left high front on Suffort on Right front armed KRUISEEKE and KOELENBERG (K31 Q1) — "B" Coy was in Divisional Reserve in trenches at GHELUVELT. Bn HQ at Sturn Central.	
	3.10.16		The 88th Bde attempts to advance the line in and around GHELUVE. Our attempt short partial of men got into the village. no forward result, own stronger and heavy casualties were suffered from Inf, Fire.	
	4.10.16		The Division was withdrawn and the Bn was accomodated as follows — HQ and Coys Sms, BEAKE CAMP (A.30.c), BCoy MC (ROZENDAAL) CCoy ACoy near ELOIE (YPRES) or Tgl DCoy Sturm Central	

A6943 Wt. W14422/M1160 350,000 12/16 D. D. & L. Forms/C/2118/14.

Army Form C. 2118.

WAR DIARY
of
INTELLIGENCE SUMMARY.
(Erase heading not required.)

Instructions regarding War Diaries and Intelligence Summaries are contained in F. S. Regs., Part II. and the Staff Manual respectively. Title pages will be prepared in manuscript.

Place	Date	Hour	Summary of Events and Information	Remarks and references to Appendices
PRESENT AREA W of YPRES	5.10.16		Warning orders (attached) were received from Division here by Division under which we are to form (subsequently) from 7th and 36th Divisions	APPENDIX A
			"C" Coy moved to Camp at Egadoro (ECOLE) and Bn: HQ was established at this camp. Warning Order to be on General reserve received	APPENDIX A
YPRES AREA	7.10.16		Continued were redistributed to Brigades and consolidated to areas as follows :-	
			A Coy (with 56th Inf Bde) Iso 20.10	
			B Coy (with 59th Inf Bde) Egado 20	
			C Coy (with 86: Inf Bde) I140 central	
			D Coy (Divisional Reserve) BRAKE CAMP	
			HQ and Bn store I9c (in above stated)	APPENDIX B
"	8-12 10.16		Owing to continuance of Divisional operations no change in dispositions took place	
			Coys remained in areas noted to their respective Brigades	

Army Form C. 2118.

WAR DIARY
INTELLIGENCE SUMMARY.
(Erase heading not required.)

Place	Date	Hour	Summary of Events and Information	Remarks and references to Appendices
Modin Busin Ru Cote	13.10.16		Coys carried forward preparatory to coming out to trenches at then Brigade to Rest Camp were thelsted. Bn RQ (5th to reserves) the D. Bn. was disposed as follows: Bn HQ @ BECCLAERE — TERRANO road at K7a 20 80. A Coy (less it amp) at J3c B " " " J6b Capt at J6b D " in dugout and shelters at C30d (BREZENBEER) C (Less 1 Coy) Town centres At other 13st moving to J5c	
LEDEGHEM SECTOR Et Coy Hut	6.10h		Chay took over the trenches from "D" Coy 10th 4th Bn MG Corps. chach ran attached to the Bn. were No 6 Battery & MOTOR MB. Bath D Coy moved up to J5c. Qm stores moved to J5c in afternoon Other Secring (ABIB) 4 the trenches now lies in LEDEGHEM through. Lis entered — K5a and atpx (Sheet 28) (Details)	APPENDIX C

Army Form C. 2118.

WAR DIARY
or
INTELLIGENCE SUMMARY.
(Erase heading not required.)

Instructions regarding War Diaries and Intelligence Summaries are contained in F. S. Regs., Part II. and the Staff Manual respectively. Title pages will be prepared in manuscript.

Place	Date	Hour	Summary of Events and Information	Remarks and references to Appendices
LEDEGHEM Sector V	14.10.18	05.35	Ready for the morning of the 10.18. A, B and D Coys moved to assembly area into their Brigade (36th, 86th and 87th respectively) C Coy remaining in Close Reserve in the line and Army Commanders (viz the 16th)	
			Battn during night 13/14 Oct. HQ Battn Mine Dyk was D Coy HQ.	
			Bn HQ Capt in was Bn in reserve.	
			At 05.35 the 29th Divn attacked in Conjunction with the 36th Divn on	APPENDIX
			the right and the 9th Divn on the left. As attack was fair	D W J*
			concealed advance of the Bn from B.D from and British Second Army. It was	
			the plan for objective was the HEULE — LEDEGHEM Railway in	
			Bn was to Co. B. 15 and 16.	
			Brigade 2nd Battn was 9th and 95th 3rd Battn (C, L and R.) but reached	
			the forward line Oct 19 1918.	
E of LEDEGHEM	15.10.18		Bn (less D Coy) was temp 0.5.95 but the 95 in Reserve at 09.00 hours	APPENDIX
			(Details later taken up by D Coy attached)	E
			He was filled HEULE — LEDEGHEM Railway on nordelen. No 6 Baking Mine	
			was formed no Bn HQ. Bn	

WAR DIARY or INTELLIGENCE SUMMARY

Army Form C. 2118.

Place	Date	Hour	Summary of Events and Information	Remarks and references to Appendices
LINE N of HEULE	5.10.18		Bty concentrated at open house and moved to billets at HARDIMOTH Cross Roads (L10d 95.95) into fighting transport. D Coy 101st Bn moved to KORTERHOEK to join 13th Bn. Own lines moved to B" HQ at K7d 3.0 5.0 (See Orders attached)	Copy APPENDIX F.
	6.10.18		Bn Bde with A Coy moved forward into support — billets in HEULE. Bg Bde held Lys-line two posts pushed to W bank of the Lys. Thrust to W. bk of Lys/Sule were cleared during the afternoon by Br Bde. D Coy from were relieved by B Coy of 59th Bn and "D" Coy moved into Reserve in SALINES. Bn HQ moved forward to L11 30.80 Own Shorts moving up to KORTERHOEK (orders attached)	APPENDIX G
	7.10.18		D Coy 101st Bn MG Coys relieved B Coy of 1st Bn in the line in own MGRMC the Company now under 80th Infantry Bde	

WAR DIARY
INTELLIGENCE SUMMARY

Army Form C. 2118.

Place	Date	Hour	Summary of Events and Information	Remarks and references to Appendices
Les Brebis (L4)	13.10.16		Reorganisation of front and adjustment of Boundaries took place in E Sector.	APPENDIX H
	16.10.16 10.16		No change in Brigade Front. "C" Company O.R. were moved into SAILLY.	
	19/20 10.16	10.14	85th Inf Bde raid to trenches of the LYS salient, forthridge on our frontage. Hove no Trenches but formed line H23c 0.0 – H15 6.2.3. There were most successfully carried out and R by moved to June camp to work all about O5.3.6 then on to O25 O2b.	
	20.10.16		At 06.00 horses left Bn retrenched to live Dog central – On Central – St Louis – T35 central 85th Bde marched to 11.13 and carried the Bn Hqts Headquarters in billets. Bn HQ moved up to AU CHEVALIER Central at H14 d 2.5 2a. 85th Bde started trench duties. Bn Hqrs line BRUAY – LES BREBIS – KOATZA Organised.	APPENDIX J.

Army Form C. 2118.

WAR DIARY
INTELLIGENCE SUMMARY.
(Erase heading not required.)

Place	Date	Hour	Summary of Events and Information	Remarks and references to Appendices
Line	20.10.18		At 5.7.3 a.m. advance was resumed towards the ESCAUT from	APPENDIX K
to R.			Against hung the line D.9 - O.9 - VICHTE - 58 (XIX Corps on our R.)	
Lys			and the D.23 - OOTEGHEM 86th Bde moved forward followed by	
			87th Bde in echelon right. 88th Bde concentrated in STACEGHEM area.	
			B Coy was relieved by E Coy in echelon to 86th Bde Bn.	
			Camp & Regtl at H.16.d.00.20 (later moved)	APPENDIX K
			Leading Bty now in action	
			HQ (forward H.16.d.00.20 (AU CHEVALIER)	
			Rear G.16.a.20.10 (SIMMES)	
			A Coy [32 central] wh: 86th Bde	
			B A.10.d.00.20 (Reserve)	
			C [25.c.25.90 (wh: 88th Bde)	
			D H.23.b.5.3 (wh: 87th Bde)	
	20.10.18		A further small advance was made by 87th Bde which pushed through	
			86th Bde but very strong resistance and heavy MG fire were	
			experienced.	

WAR DIARY
INTELLIGENCE SUMMARY

(Erase heading not required.)

Army Form C. 2118.

Place	Date	Hour	Summary of Events and Information	Remarks and references to Appendices
Line E of St LOUIS	22.10.18	—	During the advance LIEUT D.S. McGREGOR (late of D Coy) performed an exceptional act in that though he lost his life, yet his daring & great bravery enabled us to take HOOGMOLEN & BORDER Nº 11. The advance was held up, not the strong machinery gun fire coming from a house being enfilades by Cold but two Guns & limbers were set to drive across an open "no" of the Gund to a lynched road. This he did although the homes were held he and the force were fit as it enabled {....} was clearly observed Rifles obsering fire {...}	
	23/10 10.15		Mr Brown was attached by Lieut Dent in accordance with orders issued.	APPENDIX L and*
			Coys were taken with transport to {...} and dropped in {...} AC₃ (with 86ᵗʰ Bde) COERNE B C₃ (Reserve) JHb d 00.20 C C₃ (with 88ᵗʰ Bde) STREETEN D C₃ (with 87ᵗʰ Bde) MARLERESE	h

Army Form C. 2118.

WAR DIARY
or
INTELLIGENCE SUMMARY.
(Erase heading not required.)

K

Place	Date	Hour	Summary of Events and Information	Remarks and references to Appendices
COURTRAI	26-28 10.18		Division was withdrawn from the line & ceased to be in Corps. Moved by road from the Scheldt with Divisional HQ'rs stationed 25th Oct with 86th Bde from to MEUVILLE - FARRAIN and on 26th Oct to BONDUES & on 27th Oct to CROIX on 27th Oct. 87th Bde with 86th Bde first to MOUSCRON and afterwards on 28th Oct and then to CROIX on 27th Oct. 88th Bde with 87th Bde & on 28th Oct to MARCQ (overseas schools) TOURCOING and on 28th Oct to MARCQ	APPENDIX M APPENDIX N
MARCQ	29.10.18		The Battn. concentrated in MARCQ C.D and A large manoeuvre to form the Purple Green to start. They were of Reserve.	APPENDIX O

APPENDIX B

SECRET.   Copy No. 15

29th Bn. M.G.Corps Order No.31.

1. The following redistribution of Companies will come into effect as from noon tomorrow, 7th inst:-
   "B" Coy. will be attached to 87th Inf.Bde. in place of "D" Coy.
   "D" Coy. will come into Divisional Reserve.
   ("A" and "C" Coys. will remain attached to 86th and 88th Inf. Bdes. respectively.)

2. Companies will be accommodated in camps as follows:-
   "A" Coy. will remain at present location at J.5.a.50.10.
   "B" Coy. will take over camp at I.9.d.20.20. from "C" Coy.
   "C" Coy. will take over camp at J.14.a.central from "D" Coy.
   "D" Coy. will take over "B" Coy's. camp at BRAKE CAMP (A.30.c.)

3. All tentage will be left standing and handed over to incoming Company, receipts being obtained and forwarded to Battn. H.Q. Signal communications will be handed over.

4. Companies will arrange to send representatives forward to take over camps, and will clear their present locations by 9:0 a.m. Completion of moves to be wired to Battn. H.Q.

5. Q.M.Stores and Rear Battn.H.Q. as detailed, will move from BRAKE CAMP to I.9.d.20.20. tomorrow 7th inst., clearing BRAKE CAMP by 9:0 a.m. The Q.M. will send on a representative in advance.

6. The two Companies located forward (i.e. those at J.5.a. and J.14.a.) will send down for rations to new Q.M.Stores (I.9.d.20.20.) from 7th inst. The Company at J.14.a. will draw by pack animals owing to the congestion of lorry traffic on the plank road.

7. Battalion H.Q. will remain at I.9.d.20.20.

8. The Q.M. will arrange to re-issue to Companies at once any packs and blankets that have been handed in.

9. ACKNOWLEDGE.

6th October 1918.

K Macrae Moir Capn.
for Lieut.Colonel,
Comdg 29th Bn. M.G.Corps.

Copies to:
1. "A" Coy.
2. "B" "
3. "C" "
4. "D" "
5. Quartermaster.
6. Signals Officer.
7. 29th Div."B"
8. 29th Div. "A".
9. 86th Inf.Bde.
10. 87th " "
11. 88th " "
12. 1st Motor M.G.Bde.
13. 104th Bn. M.G.Corps.
14. File.
15. War Diary.

S E C R E T.   Appendix C.
Copy No. 12

20th Bn. M.G. CORPS.
Administrative Instructions No. 4.

1. **SUPPLIES.**

   (a)   Rations for consumption on J day will be carried on the men.
   "A", "B", "C" and "D" Coys., "D" Coy. 104th Bn. M.G.Corps, and No.6 Battery M.M.G.Bde will send the necessary transport to Q.M. Stores (I.15.d.20.66.) by 9:0 a.m. on J minus 1 day to draw these rations.

   (b)   On the afternoon of J minus 1 day the Q.M. Stores and Rear Battalion H.Q. will move forward to J.5.c.30.80. (vicinity of "A" Coy.)

   (c)   Rations for consumption on J plus 1 day will be drawn by Companies and attached units from the Q.M. Stores at J.5.c.30.80. on J day by 11 a.m.

2. **BLANKETS & PACKS.**

   All Companies will wear Fighting order. Greatcoats will be carried on the fighting limbers.
   Blankets and packs will be dumped at the Q.M. Stores at J.5.c.30.80. between 5 and 7 p.m.

3. **PACK SADDLES.**

   All Companies will maintain 24 pack saddles as follows :-

	Fighting	Rations
"A" Coy.	16	8
"B" "	16	8
"C" "	16	8
"D" "	16	8

   Of the 32 pack saddles in possession of "C" Coy., two will be handed over to "B" Coy. and remaining six handed in to Q.M. Stores at J.5.c.30.80.

12th October 1918.   Major,
                                            Comdg 20th Bn. M.G.Corps.

Copies to: 1. "A" Coy.   7. No. 6 Bty.M.M.G.Bde.
             2. "B" "   8. Quartermaster.
             3. "C" "   Fwd.   9. Signals.
             4. "C" "   Rear.   10. File
             5. "D" Coy.   11.)
             6. "D" Coy. 104th Bn. 12.) War Diary.

APPENDIX F.

SECRET.   Copy No. 16

29th Bn. M.G. CORPS.
Operation Order No. 35.

Reference maps: Sheets 28 and 29.

1. "C" Coy. 29th Bn. M.G.Corps will concentrate tomorrow morning 15th inst. and move with fighting transport to the vicinity of HARDMOUTH CROSS ROADS (L.10.d.95.95.). The Company will clear present area by 09.00 hours. Completion of move and exact location to be reported to Battn.Headquarters.
    The Section of "D" Coy. 104th Bn. M.G.Corps attached to "C" Coy. will not move forward, but will concentrate in the vicinity of present "C" Coy. Headquarters, KANTERHOEK.

2. No.6 Battery, 1st Motor M.G. Bde. will move at 05.00 hours tomorrow 15th inst. from present location to vicinity of PENNY CORNER in L.18.d. via DADIZEELE and LEDEGHEM. On arrival at this point, O.C. Battery will report to G.O.C. 87th Inf.Bde, in Brigade concentration area in L.12.central. Final location to be reported to Battalion Headquarters. The Battery will move with it the eight bivouacs already issued.

3. "D" Coy. 104th Bn. M.G.Corps will move from present location at 10.00 hours tomorrow 15th inst. to KANTERHOEK (K.12.b.90.80.).
    Route :-   Cross Roads J.12.d.2.6. - TERHAND - DADIZEELE.
    (The road through K.8.c. and d. and K.9 and K.4. is at present impassable for lorries).
    On arrival at KANTERHOEK, O.C. Coy. will report at new Battn. Headquarters for exact location to which to proceed.
    The Company will move with it the sixteen bivouacs already issued.

4. Q.M. Stores, Rear Battn.Headquarters, all Company Rear H.Q. and transport, and ten per cent personnel will move from present location at 11.00 hours tomorrow 15th inst. to K.7.d.3.8. (present Battn. Headquarters).

5. Forward Battn.Headquarters will close at present location at 09.00 hours tomorrow 15th inst. and re-open at same hour at L.7.a.1.6. (KANTERHOEK).

6. ACKNOWLEDGE.

14th October 1918.   Major,
                                        Comdg 29th Bn. M.G.Corps.

Copies to:
1. "A" Coy. Forward.)
2. "B" "   "   ) for
3. "D" "   "   ) information
4. "C" Coy. Forward.
5. "A" Coy. Rear.
6. "B" "   "
7. "C" "   "
8. "D" "   "
9. Quartermaster.
10. No.6 Bty. 1st M.M.G.Bde.
11. 29th Division G.
12. 87th Inf. Bde.
13.) File.
14.)
15.) War Diary.
16.)
17. "D" Coy. 104th Bn. M.G.C.

SECRET.   APPENDIX LX.   Copy No. 8

29th Bn. M.G.CORPS.

Operation Order No. 36.

Reference sheet 29.

1. The 29th Division is being relived tonight 23/24th inst. by the 41st Division.

2. On relief Companies will move with Brigades into billeting areas.
   The Battalion will then be disposed as follows :-

   ```
   Battn.H.Q.   -   H.16.d.00.20.
   "A" Coy.     -   CUERNE (with 86th Bde)
   "B"  "       -   H.16.d.00.20. (in Reserve)
   "C"  " )     -   STEENBRUGGE-STACEGHEM Area (with 88th and
   "D"  " )     -        87th Bdes respectively).
   ```

3. Companies will notify Battn.H.Q.(by runner direct) their exact location as soon as possible.
   They will at once get into signal communication with Brigades.

4. The Q.M.Stores is moving to a location in square H.8. this afternoon. Exact location will be wired to Coys.

5. Coy.Rear H.Q., 10% personnel and Transport of "A" and "D" Coys. will join their Coys. forthwith under arrangements to be made by O.C. Coys.

6. ACKNOWLEDGE.

23rd October 1918.   Major,
                                            Comdg 29th Bn. M.G.Corps.

```
Copies to:   1. "A" Coy.     5.) War Diary
             2. "B"  "       6.)
             3. "C"  "       7.) File.
             4. "D"  "       8.)
```

SECRET.   APPENDIX N.   Copy No. 6

29th Bn. M.G.CORPS.
Operation Order No. 57.

Ref: 1:40,000 Sheet 29.
     TOURNAI 5.

1. Battn.H.Q., "B" and "D" Coys. will move tomorrow 27th inst. with 87th Bde. Group to the area W. of MOUSCRON.

2. Battn. H.Q., "B" and "D" Coys. will form up in column of route in order named on main HARLEBEKE - COURTRAI road facing S.W. head of column being at road junction H.16.c.95.00. Column will be ready to move at 08.25 hours.

3. Q.M.Stores and remainder of H.Q. Transport will form up in column of route at same starting point and time facing N.E. and will join column immediately behind Battn.H.Q. on moving off.

4. The strictest attention will be paid to march discipline, both of personnel and vehicles. Companies will march in the normal M.G. Battn. Formation (i.e. each sub-section behind its own limber). Intervals of 100 yards will be maintained between Companies. Men will wear caps, and greatcoats will be carried in packs. Blankets will be carried on limbers.

5. Dinners - on arrival. A haversack ration will be carried on the man.

6. Billeting parties will proceed in advance as follows :-
One officer (mounted) and two cyclists per Company. Three cyclists from Battn.H.Q. (The "B" Coy. Billeting Officer will be responsible for finding Battn.H.Q. billets).
Above parties will report to Staff Captain 87th Bde. at cross roads just N. of TOURCOING between VIEILLE MOTTE and CHENE HOUPLINE (X.25.a.95.50.) at 09.30 hours. They will meet Battalion at cross roads at tenth Kilo. stone on COURTRAI - TOURCOING road (S.8.b.95.55.).

7. On the 28th inst. Battn.H.Q. and "B" Coy. will move independently to MAROQ, and "D" Coy. will move with 87th Bde. to ST. ANDRE.
Instructions for these moves will be issued later.

8. "B" and "D" Coys. are being rationed through 87th Inf.Bde. from consumption 26th inst. and will arrange to draw direct on arrival on 27th inst.

9. Battn.H.Q. closes at present location at 08.00 hours 27th inst. and re-opens in new area on arrival. Location will be notified later.

10. Companies and Q.M. to ACKNOWLEDGE.

26th October 1918.

                                   Lieut.Colonel,
                              Comdg. 29th Bn. M.G.Corps.

Copies to: 1. "B" Coy.   4. 87th Bde. (for information).
            2. "D" "   5 & 6. War Diary.
            3. Q.M.   7. File.

War Diary.
November 1st – 30th – 1918.

29th Battn – Machine Gun Corps –

WAR DIARY or INTELLIGENCE SUMMARY

Army Form C. 2118.

Place	Date	Hour	Summary of Events and Information	Remarks and references to Appendices
MARCKE Klo-Kilo	1.11.18		Battalion in billets. During evening which enclosed 1 hour per day practice for Exercise Bush. Ammunition drill & gas drills for all R's under Plat Serg. Majors. Sports in afternoon.	
do.	2.11.18		Inspection by XI Corps Commander. March post with limbers.	
do.	3.11.18		Training (Machine Gun) at Company HHQs. Sports in afternoon.	
do.	4.11.18		Battalion (Coy. "C" Coy) Machine Gun Gunnery at Coy HHQs. L. Coy move with 88th Inf. Bde to TOMBROEK (Hq - Tuter).	
do.	5.11.18		Batt- carries out training. "C" Coy (with 88th Bde) take over M.G. Sector from 11.30 central to N15d 00. 2 sectors reliens 6 guns of 14th Bath MGC. On the right and 1 section relieves 4 guns of the 3rd Batt MGC on left. The remaining section kept in reserve at V6a5 (Sheet 28).	App 1
do.	6.11.18		Battn (less "C" Coy) move with 86th Bde to billets at WIJNGHE (Hq - Buy) Coy. In accordance with	App 2
do.	7.11.18		29th Div. Open- Order No.1 - 88th Bde Order No.222 - 2 Section of "C" Coy Cross the R. SCHELDT	App 3 & 4
WIJNGHE	8.11.18		"B" Coy from 87th Inf Bde moved to billets at 29a 32 b5. "C" Coy (less 1 sec) Diencien	App 5

A6945 Wt. W1442/M1160 350,000 12/16 D. D. & L. Forms/C./2118/14.

WAR DIARY
or
INTELLIGENCE SUMMARY

Army Form C. 2118.

Place	Date	Hour	Summary of Events and Information	Remarks and references to Appendices
ST. SAUVEUR. SL39/F2L9	16/11/18		Moving with 88th Bde. reach SAINT SAUVEUR. F2L9. (about 37) Batt. H.Q. and "A" D Coy. march with 88 Bde. to billets at PETIT TOURCOING. (about 29. T10d.)	App 6.
CELLES (SL31/D16) ST GENOIS			"C" Coy (with 88th Bde) at ST. SAUVEUR. at F2L9. "B" Coy. with 89th Bde. in Support reach CELLES & billet at 37/D18a. Bgn. H.Q. with "A" and "D" Coys. Bn move by march route to ST. GENOIS 31/G19a.	Appx 7
	17/11/18 08 00		"B" Coy move forward to establish a line of outposts on the R.DENDRE and at the time the Armistice commenced had reached HESSINES. "B" Coy remained at CELLES and Batt. H.Q. with "A" "D" Coys remained at ST GENOIS. The day was spent in general cleaning up.	
ST. GENOIS	18/11/18		Batt "A" Coy and "D" Coy remain in billets at ST GENOIS. "B" Coy at CELLES. "C" Coy at HESSINES. One Lt. section in position at BRIDGE on R.DENDRE at 38/C17a28.	
CELLES SL31/D16	19/11/18		Battalion less "B" "C" Coys move by march route to billets at CELLES SL31/D16A.	

At 9943 Wt. W11442/M1160 350,000 12/16 D. D. & L. Forms/C/2118/14.

WAR DIARY
or
INTELLIGENCE SUMMARY.

(Erase heading not required.)

Army Form C. 2118.

Place	Date	Hour	Summary of Events and Information	Remarks and references to Appendices
FLOBECQ. Sh.30/T27.	14/11/18		in accordance with 29th Divl. Order No 291. GHQ. (Sheet 30/V26c centre). Battn. (less B Coy) marched to FLOBECQ Sh.30/T27 centre — "B" Coy at GHOY. — "C" Coy at LESSINES.	"B" Coy note to N. of App 6.
LESSINES. Sh.38/C16	15/11/18		The whole Battalion concentrated in LESSINES, proceeding to billets there by march route, "B" Coy moving independently.	(9.)
LESSINES	16/11/18		Preparing for march eastward. Bathing and cleaning up.	
ENGHIEN. Sh.38/F26.	16/11/18		Battalion moved with 88th Bde by march route to ENGHIEN. 2 sections of "C" Coy join 4th Worcest. Regt. to proceed as Advanced Guard to Brigade.	App 10 & 11
ENGHIEN	19/11/18 20/11/18		Training at Captns billets.	
BRAINE-LE CHATEAU. (Brussels 6.) (A.D.)	21/11/18		Batt. (less "C" Coy) march to BRAINE LE CHATEAU. — "C" Coy from 89th Bde at I TTRE. (Waterloo 6. (SD))	App 12
-do-	22/11/18		Batt. (less "C" Coy) 10a.m. at Braine-le Chateau, resting & cleaning.	

WAR DIARY
or
INTELLIGENCE SUMMARY

Army Form C. 2118.

(Erase heading not required.)

Instructions regarding War Diaries and Intelligence Summaries are contained in F. S. Regs., Part II. and the Staff Manual respectively. Title pages will be prepared in manuscript.

Place	Date	Hour	Summary of Events and Information	Remarks and references to Appendices
OHAIN. (Brussels 6.) A.F.	23/11/18		The march to the frontier is continued, the Battn. (less "C"Coy) moving to billets at OHAIN. "C" Coy move to vicinity of FORM - 1 MILE N.W. of B. on BOUSVAL (Sheet BRUSSELS 6 - 5.G.)	13.
— do —	24/11/18		All Officers & NCOs ride to WATERLOO where the Brigadier Officer addresses them, briefly relating the history of the battle. "C" Coy move to BLANMONT. (Sheet Brussels 6 - 5.H.)	14
CEROUX MOUSTY. (Sh. BRUSSELS 6.) 5.G.	25/11/18		The march East is continued, the Batt.n (less "C" Coy) marching to CEROUX - MOUSTY.	
CORBAIS. Sh. Brussels 6 (ft.16/18) 5.H.	26/11/18		Battalion forced by march route to billets at CORBAIS via MOUSTY - COURT ST ETIENNE - MONT ST GUIBERT. and join 86th Bde.	15
LONGCHAMPS (Sh. Brussels 6.) 6.K.	27/11/18		The advance is continued with 86th Bde to LONGCHAMPS - "C"Coy with 87th Bde. rejoin CORTIL-WODEN (Sh. BRUSSELS 6 - 6.L) Batt. (less "C"Coy) move to ANTHEIT, marching via L'ANGLE - FORVILLE	16
ANTHEIT. (Sh. LIEGE 7.) 6C.	28/11/18		BIERWART. — "C" Coy march with 87th Bde to billets at LES COMMUNES. (Sheet HANNUT LIEGE - 6.D.)	17.

Army Form C. 2118.

WAR DIARY
or
INTELLIGENCE SUMMARY.
(Erase heading not required.)

Instructions regarding War Diaries and Intelligence Summaries are contained in F. S. Regs., Part II. and the Staff Manual respectively. Title pages will be prepared in manuscript.

Place	Date	Hour	Summary of Events and Information	Remarks and references to Appendices
FRAITURE (de MARCHE) 1 F.	29/11/18		(low cloud) The Bn proceeded with 86th Bde by March route to billets at FRAITURE. "C" Coy with 89th Bde march to COMBLAIN-FAIRON (de MARCHE - 1G)	H.
REMOUCHAMPS (de MARCHE) 1 I.	30/11/18		The Bn march to continue, The Batt: (less Coy) reaching REMOUCHAMPS. "C" Coy march with 89th Bde to billets in vicinity of HALT, 2 miles W of SPA. (de MARCHE - 1K.)	18.

Appendix I

SECRET.

Copy No. 24

29th DIVISION ORDER No. 288.

Map references, 1/40,000.
Sheets 29, 36 & 37.

6th November 1918.

1. On transfer from XV to X Corps the 29th Division (less 88th Infantry Brigade Group) will move to-morrow Nov. 7th, and Nov. 8th, by March Route in accordance with March Table attached.

2. Brigade Groups will be composed as under.-

86th Brigade Group.	87th Brigade Group.
86th Inf. Bde.	87th Inf. Bde.
29th Bn. M.G.C. (Less "C" Co.)	1/2 Monmouth R. (P).
89th Field Ambulance.	510th Field Co. R.E.
No. 2 Co. Div. Train.	455 Field Co. R.E.
	87th Field Ambulance.
	No. 3 Co. Div. Train.

3. All billeting accommodation will be allotted by 29th Div."Q".

4. Divisional H.Q. will close at present location at 10.00. Nov. 7th, at which hour it will re-open at ROLLEGHEM.

5. Completion of moves and new locations to be notified to this office.

6. ACKNOWLEDGE.

G. Heffernan Major GS
for Lieut-Colonel
General Staff, 29th Division.

Issued at 15.30.

Distribution.

	Copy No.		Copy No.
G.O.C.	1	D.A.D.O.S.	29
G.S.	2- 5	Camp Comdt.	30
"Q"	6- 7	29th Div. M.T. Co.	31
C.R.A.	8-14	226 Div. Emp. Co.	32
C.R.E.	15	Div. Gas Offr.	33
Signals.	16	Div. Reception Camp.	34
86th Inf. Bde.	17-18	French Mission.	35
87th Inf. Bde.	19-20	Belgian Mission.	36
88th Inf. Bde.	21-22	XV Corps.	37-38
1/2 Monmouth R. (P)	23	-do- R.A.	39
29th Bn. M.G.Corps.	24	-do- R.A.	40
Div. Train.	25	X Corps.	41-42
A.D.M.S.	26	14th Division.	43
D.A.D.V.S.	27	30th Division.	44
D.A.P.M.	28	War Diary.	45-46

M A R C H T A B L E.

Unit	Date	From	To	Route	Remarks.
85th Brigade Group.	Nov. 8th.	BONDUES.	LUINGHE	BONDUES - Cross-roads E.7.d.5.7. - TURCOING - MOUSCRON.	Not to cross HOUSCRON - LAUWE railway before 1145.
87th Brigade Group.	Nov. 7th.	ST. ANDRE.	TURCOING.	WAMBRECHIES - Cross-roads E.29. c.4.2. - BONDUES - Cross-roads E.7.d.50.75.	Take over vacated billets of Divl. Artillery, not to arrive at Cross-roads E.7. d.50.75. before 1030.
	Nov. 8th.	TURCOING.	Area T.4. T.5. T.8. T.9. T.10. T.11. T.12.	MOUSCRON - LUINGHE.	To billets vacated by 85th Inf.Bde. To be East of MOUSCRON - LAUWE railway by 1130.
29th Div. Artillery.	Nov. 7th.	TURCOING.	T.13,14,15 and 13.	MOUSCRON - LUINGHE.	To be clear of TURCOING by 1030. Traffic regulations to be observed as laid down in S.S.724.
29th Div. Headqtrs.	Nov. 7th.	NOUVEAUX.	ROLLEGHEM.	TURCOING - AELBEKE.	To be clear of TURCOING 1030.

Appendix

SECRET.
COPY NO. 16.

88th Infantry Brigade Order No. 221.

Reference Sheet 28 1/40,000.   7th November, 1918.

1. The 88th Inf. Bde. will take over the front from U.30.c.central to V.14.d.0.0. on the 7th and night 7th/8th November as follows:-

   (a) From the 41st Inf. Bde., 14th Division, from U.30.c.central to U.24.d.6.3.

   (b) From 89th Inf. Bde., 30th Division, from U.24.d.6.3. to V.14.d.0.0.

2. (a) The 4th Worcestershire Regt will take over the Right Sector of the front from U.30.c.central to U.24.d.6.3. and will take over from 29th D.L.I. H.Q. at U.22.c.1.8.
   They will relieve only one Coy of this Battn, which holds posts between L'ESCAUT and the GRAND COURANT. Guides will meet this Coy at U.11.a.0.6. at 1830, who will be accompanied by an officer who knows the strength and position of the posts.
   The remainder of the Battn will be disposed as follows:-

   Battn H.Q. U.10.c.3.6.
   One Coy in U.16.d.
   Two Coys in U.9.

   (b) The 2nd Leinster Regt will take over the Left Sector of the front from the 2/16th London Regt. H.Q. U.6.a.3.5.
   They will relieve two Coys only of this Battn:-
   One Coy along the road in U.18.d. and U.13.c.
   One Coy in U.10.b.

   Guides will be at U.11.a.0.6. at 1700.
   The remainder of the Battn will be disposed as follows:-

   Battn H.Q. O.32.d.8.0.
   Two Coys in O.32. and 33.

   (c) The 88th T.M.Bty. will relieve two Trench Mortars in the Right Sector. These guns will come under the tactical command of O.C. 4th Worcestershire Regt.

   (d) O.C. "C" Coy, 29th M.G.Bn., will arrange to relieve 8 guns in the Right Sector and 4 guns in the Left Sector, and will keep the remaining 4 guns in Support. He will send a representative to arrange details to H.Q. 41st Inf. Bde., B.5.a.4.8., at 1000 and to H.Q. 89th Inf. Bde., O.23.a.5.6., at 1200.
   Guns at present in the line which are not relieved are to be withdrawn at midnight.

3. Details of Relief will be arranged between Commanding Officers concerned.
   Reliefs in back areas will be carried out in daylight.

4. Route for Coys relieving in the forward area:-

   T.5.b.3.6. - U.1.a.5.7. - U.31.c.8.2. -
   DRIES - U.11.a.0.6.

5. Cookers will accompany all Coys except those in the front areas.

6. Billeting parties will report to Brigade H.Q. as under:-
   4th Worcestershire Regt - 0830.
   2nd Leinster Regt - 0900.

7. 1st Line transport will remain in its present billets.

-2-

8. Any Stores of ammunition etc. that may exist will be taken over and location and size of dump will be reported to these H.Q.

9. Completion of Relief will be reported to these H.Q. by the use of the Code word "DUMPS".

10. Command of the Sector will pass to G.O.C. 88th Inf. Bde. upon completion of Relief.

11. Brigade H.Q. will close at its present location, and will open at GAAI SAPT, C.32.b.7.1., at 1700.

12. ACKNOWLEDGE.

F. S. Williams
Captain,
Brigade Major, 88th Infantry Brigade.

Issued at 0700

Copies to 1 - 4 Staff.
5 4th Worcestershire Regt.
6 2nd Hampshire Regt.
7 2nd Leinster Regt.
8 88th Trench M. Bty.
9 "C" Coy, 29th M.G.Bn.
10 497th Fd. Coy, R.E.
11 88th Fd. Amb.
12 86th Inf. Bde.
13 87th Inf. Bde.
14 29th Div. "G".
15 29th D.A.
16 29th Bn. M.G.Corps.
17 41st Inf. Bde.
18 89th Inf. Bde.
19 58th Bde A.F.A.
20 File.
21 Diary.

SECRET.   29th Div. No. C.G.S.61/171.
****

Appendix 3

29th DIVISION OPERATIONS INSTRUCTION No.1

Ref: 1/40,000   8th November 1918

1. The 29th Division is to be prepared to force the crossing of the ESCAUT on a date "J" day and at an hour "H" hour which will be notified later. Preparations are to be completed by the 10th inst. On our Right the 14th Division of the XV Corps and on our Left the 30th Division of the X Corps are forcing a crossing at the same time.

2. Boundaries and objectives for the 29th Division are shown on attached trace "A".
    The first objective will be the line High Ground D.20.b. - CELLES (incl) - CARNOY (excl). From this a further advance will be made to the second objective the Division advancing with its Right on the general line LA BACOTTERIE (incl) - Road Junction (J.5.c.) - DELPRE - High Ground K.2.a.

3. The 29th Division attack will be carried out by the 88th Infantry Brigade. 87th Brigade will be Support and 86th Brigade Reserve Brigade.

4. In preparation for this 88th Brigade will by the morning of the 10th clear the enemy from the West bank of the GRAND COURANT and establish posts on that line.

5.(a) On I/J night footbridges and if possible packbridges will be thrown over the GRAND COURANT by which 88th Brigade will cross between 01.00 and 06.00 hours on J. day and be formed up ready to advance under a creeping barrage to the 1st objective.

   (b) This barrage will make its first lift at H. plus 5 minutes from a line about 300 yards east of the River.
    The pace of the barrage will be 100 yards in 3 minutes with a pause of 10 minutes at approximately every 1,000 yards.

6. 87th Brigade in support will cross the River as soon as the advance has got well started, and will be prepared to leapfrog the 88th Infantry Brigade on the line of the 1st objective.

7. ACKNOWLEDGE.

                                                    Lieut-Colonel, G.S.
                                                        29th Division.

86th Inf. Bde.   A.D.M.S.
87th Inf. Bde.   29th Bn. M.G. Corps.
88th Inf. Bde.   "Q".
C.R.A.   14th Division.
C.R.E.   30th Division.
Signals.   X Corps.

B.

Appendix A

SECRET.
COPY NO. 16

88th Infantry Brigade Order No. 222.

Reference Sheet 29.   8th November, 1918.

1. The 29th Division, in conjunction with the Divisions on the Right and Left, will force the crossing of the SCHELDT at a date to be notified later.

2. The 88th Brigade will attack on the 29th Divisional front. Preparations for the attack will be complete by the 10th.

3. Prior to the major operation, the following minor operations will take place:-

(a) 1. On the night of the 8th/9th November the 2nd Leinster Regt will move one Coy across L'ESCAUT, and establish posts on the left of the 4th Worcestershire Regt, covering the remainder of the front as far as our Left boundary. For this purpose they will have priority of movement over Bridge No. 2 (U.24.B.7.7) and the use of the ferry in vicinity of U.13.c.30.05.

As soon as the far bank is reported free of the enemy, the 497th Field Coy will construct another infantry bridge near the ferry. For this purpose the R.E. officer will work direct with the O.C. 2nd Leinster Regt.

2. One section of "C" Coy, 29/M.G.Bn., will relieve two platoons of the 4th Worcestershire Regt across L'ESCAUT. These platoons will retire into rest billets. The arrangements will be made between O.Cs. 4th Worcestershire Regt and O.C. "C" Coy, 29/M.G.Bn.

The M.Gs. will come under the tactical command of O.C. 4th Worcestershire Regt.

3. Vigorous patrolling will be carried out between L'ESCAUT and the GRAND COURANT on the whole of the Brigade front. Patrols will carry out these operations undetected, if possible, but will give fight if the enemy are met with on our side of the GRAND COURANT.

O.C. 4th Worcestershire Regt will send out a patrol to examine the bridge over the GRAND COURANT. O.C. 497th Field Coy, R.E. will attach sapper personnel to this patrol for the purpose of destroying any enemy demolition charges that may exist.

(b) 1. On the night of the 9th/10th November, the 2nd Hampshire Regt will take over with one Coy the centre sector of the defence from elements of the 4th Worcestershire and 2nd Leinster Regts. Allocation of bridges on night 9th/10th:-

No. 1, U.30.a.9.3., - 4th Worcestershire Regt.
No. 2, U.24.B.7.7., - 2nd Hampshire Regt.
No. 3, near ferry in U.13.c. - 2nd Leinster Regt.

2. One section of "C" Coy, 29th M.G.Bn. will move across L'ESCAUT to that portion of the sector held by the 2nd Leinster Regt.

M.Gs. will be redistributed when the 2nd Hampshire Regt take over. Command of M.Gs. will then pass to O.C. Sectors.

Note. Two sections will then be across the river.

3. Two platoons of the 2nd Leinster Regt will be withdrawn across L'ESCAUT and move into billets.

4. Each Battn will establish two posts at dusk on the North-West bank of the GRAND COURANT. These posts will remain out by day, if possible, but should the tactical situation not permit of their

-2-

staying out they will be withdrawn before dawn.

<u>Note.</u>   It is of the utmost importance that no infantry activity should be discovered prior to the attack.

3.   Os.C. Units will take steps to ensure a thourough reconnaissance of the ground between L'ESCAUT and the GRAND COURANT, with a view to the furture assembly in this area.

4.   Brigade Units to ACKNOWLEDGE.

F.S. Whinney
Captain,

Issued at 1230.   Brigade Major, 88th Infantry Brigade.

Copies to:

    1-4 Staff.
    5 4th Worcestershire Regt.
    6 2nd Hampshire Regt.
    7 2nd Leinster Regt.
    8 88th Trench M. Bty.
    9 "C" Coy, 29/M.G.Bn.
    10 497th Fd. Coy. R.E.
    11 29th Div. Arty.
    12 29th Div. "G".
    13 88th Fd. Ambce.
    14 41st Inf. Bde.
    15 89th Inf. Bde.
    16 29th M.G.Bn.
    17 C.R.E. 29th Div.
    18 38th Army Brigade R.F.A.
    19 86th Inf. Bde.
    20 87th Inf. Bde.
    21 Staff Capt, Rear.
    22 File.
    23 Diary.

"C" FORM.
MESSAGES AND SIGNALS. Army Form C.
No. of Message

Prefix	Code	Words	Sent, or sent out.	Office Stamp.
Received from	By		At ___ m.	
Service Instructions			To ___ By	

Handed in at ___ Office 1"37 m. Received ___ m.

TO 29 M.G. Bn.

Sender's Number.	Day of Month.	In reply to Number.	A A A
G 868			
88	Bde	will	cross
the	river	ESCAUT	at
once	and	Folly	moves
will	take	place	at
once	and	87	Bde
to	area	vacated	by
88	Bde	and	86
Bde.	group	to	area
vacated	by	87	Bde
off	29	m.	g
Bn	will	detail	one
co	to	join	87
Bde	at	once	two

FROM
PLACE & TIME

"C" FORM.
MESSAGES AND SIGNALS.

Prefix	Code	Words	Sent, or sent out.	Office Stamp.
Received from	By		At ... m.	
Service Instructions			To	
			By	

Handed in at .... Office 1137 m. Received 1140 m.

TO — (2)

*Sender's Number.	Day of Month.	In reply to Number.	A A A
17	hde	RFA	will
move	to	ST GENOIS	and
be	ready	to	cross
river	at	HELEMIN	as
soon	as	bridge	is
complete	aaa	Added	CRa
96	87	88	ldes
26	Bu	mg corps	and
1"Q"	sectd	110	Corps
14th	add	30	divs

FROM — 3y Div
PLACE & TIME

* This line, except A A A, should be erased, if not required.

Prefix	Code 750	Words 46	Sent, or sent out	Office Stamp
Received from YBI By Rem			At m.	
Service Instructions			To:	Appendix
Msg Op PT7			By	6
Handed in at YBI		Office 750 m. Received m.		

TO 29 MG Bn

Sender's Number	Day of Month	In reply to Number	AAA
GS877	9		
In	continuation	of	GS868
of	9th	inst	88th
Bde	has	crossed	the
ESCAUT	and	reached	the
line	of	the	second
objective	approximately	E16	E27
& E26	das	Advance	will
be	continued	tomorrow	0900
aaa	88th	Bde	to
which	are	attached	'A'
Squadron	7th	DG's	and
XI	Corps	Cyclist	Bn
will	advance	due	east
with	objective	the	high

FROM

PLACE & TIME

MESSAGES AND SIGNALS

Prefix	Code	Words	Sent, or sent out. At ___ m.	Office Stamp
Received from	By Runner		To	
Service Instructions Urgt of PSY			By	

Handed in at Y01 Office 1750 m. Received 1812 m.

TO (2)

Sender's Number	Day of Month	In reply to Number	AAA
CS877	9		
ground	on	F18	and
F24	aaa	87th	Bde
will	cross	the	ESCAUT
at	0800	and	move
forward	as	support	Bde
towards	the	CELLES	area
aaa	86	Bde	will
move	at	0800	to
the	ROOKERSHOEK BOSSUYT		area
and	be	in	divnl
reserve	17th	Bde	RFA
will	cross	the	ESCAUT
at	HELCHIN	when	bridging
facilities	admit	and	support

FROM

PLACE & TIME

MESSAGES AND ...

Prefix	Code	Words	Sent, or sent out.	Office Stamp
Received from	By		At ___ m.	
Service Instructions			To ___	
	Urgt Ops PTY		By	

Handed in at ___ Office 1750 m. Received 1812 m.

TO ___ (3) ___

Sender's Number.	Day of Month.	In reply to Number.	AAA
GS877	9		

the advance of 98th
Bde aaa Advd Dvnl
Report Centry has been
established at Bossuyt chateau
V18d58 aaa Acknowledge aaa
Added all concerned

FROM ___ 99 Bn G ___
PLACE & TIME ___ 1735

Appendix 7

"C" FORM.
MESSAGES AND SIGNALS.

TO: 29 M.I.B.

Sender's Number	Day of Month	In reply to Number	AAA
88	Bde	have	moved
today	reached	line	425
with	A10	with	their
Cavalry	on	line of	
the	road	Basanth	Both
advance	will	be	continued
at	0600	tomorrow	by
88	Bde	Group	who
will	establish	a	line
of	outposts	on	their
Dehore	from	say	with
to	611659	aaa	cavalry
will	be	sent	on
to	seize	crossings	over

FROM

PLACE & TIME

"C" FORM.
MESSAGES AND SIGNALS.

Prefix	Code	Words	Sent, or sent out.	Office Stamp
Received from	By		At m.	XI. 13. C
Service Instructions			To	SIGNALS
			By	

Handed in at .... Office .... m. Received .... m.

TO 2

Sender's Number.	Day of Month.	In reply to Number.	AAA
JW27	10		
DENDRE	and	prevent	their
destruction	by	enemy	aaa
The	left	of	74
Divn	is	to	be
established	at	LAHAMIDE	B26
where	88	Bde	will
gain	touch	with	their
by	mounted	troops	aaa
87	Bde	will	move
at	0900	as	support
Brigade	to	the	SAINT
SAUVEUR	area	aaa	86
Bde	and	Divn	Arty
less	17	Bde	RFA

FROM

PLACE & TIME

"C" FORM.
MESSAGES AND SIGNALS.

Prefix	Code	Words	Sent, or sent out.	Office Stamp.
Received from 2045	By		At	
Service Instructions			To	
			By	

Handed in at .... Office .... m. Received .... m.

TO 3

Sender's Number.	Day of Month.	In reply to Number.	AAA
GW 207			

Will remain in reserve West of the SCHELDT aaa 29 Div HQ moves tomorrow from GENNES to SAINT SAUVEUR and 30 Div HQ are at WATRIPONT at E5b aaa acknowledge add to all concerned

FROM 29 Divn
PLACE & TIME 2045

Appendix 8.

SECRET.　　　　　　　　　　　　　29th Division No. G.S.S 67/172.

WARNING ORDER.

29th Division complete will concentrate in an area E. of the line S.13.c.0.0. - A.24.c.00. and will take over the front now held by 70th Division. 30th Division (less infantry brigade and artillery west of ESCAUT will concentrate in area west of above line and east of River RHOSNES. X Corps Cyclist Battalion will be attached to 30th Division from 1600 to-morrow and will move into area allotted to 70th Division. Above moves to be completed by 1800 hours on 14th. 7th Dragoon Guards will on completion be attached to 29th Division.

　　　　　　　　　　　　　　　　　　　[signature]
Issued at 2000.　　　　　　　　　　　　　Lieut-Col,
12/11/1918.　　　　　　　　　　　General Staff, 29th Division.

Copies to
　　"Q"　　　　　　　　D.A.D.V.S.
　　C.R.A.　　　　　　　D.A.P.M.
　　C.R.E.　　　　　　　D.A.D.O.S.
　　Signals　　　　　　Camp Comdt.
　　86th Inf. Bde.　　29th Div. M.T. Co.
　　87th Inf. Bde.　　226 Div. Emp. Co.
　　88th Inf. Bde.　　Div Gas Offr.
　　1/2 Mon. Regt.　　Belgian Mission.
　　29th Bn. M.G.C　　X Corps.
　　Train.　　　　　　30th Div.
　　A.D.M.S.　　　　　74th Division.

SECRET.   Copy No. 24

29th DIVISION ORDER No. 291.

13th November 1918.

Ref.1/40,000. Sheets
20, 30, 37, 38.

1. The Division will concentrate in the area EAST of a line through S.18.c.0.0. - A.24.c.0.0. tomorrow, in accordance with attached March Table.

2. 88th Inf.Bde. will establish posts on all crossings over the River DENDRE as far North as V.15.a.2.5. by 1000, 14th Nov.

3. Billeting areas are allotted as follows :-
   86th Bde.Group.   T.13,14,19,20,25,26. I.1.2.7.8.
   87th Bde. Group. T.30, L.6 & 12, U.19,20,21,25,26,27, O.1,2 & 3.
   88th Bde.Group.   O.22 & 23,   16,17,10,11,12,5 & 6,
                     U.29,30,23,24,17,18.
   R.A. Group.   B.9.,10,15,16,21,22.
   1/2 Mon.R.(P).   FLOBECQ.

4. Brigade Groups are constituted as follows :-

86th Brigade Group.	87th Brigade Group.	88th Bde. Group.
86th Inf.Bde.	87th Inf.Bde.	88th Inf.Bde.
1 Coy.29th Bn.M.G.Corps.	1 Coy.29 Bn.M.G.C.	1 Coy.Bn.M.G.C.
510th Field Coy.,R.E.)	455th Field Coy.R.E.)	497th Fd.Coy.,
(B.30.b.7.5.))	(F.20.c.4.4.).)	R.E.
No.2 Coy. Train.	No.3 Coy.Train.	No.4 Coy.Train.
89th Field Ambce.	87th Field Ambce.	88th Fd. Ambce.

R.A.Group.
15th Bde. R.H.A.
17th Bde. R.F.A.

No.1 Coy.Train.

5. Divisional Headquarters will close at ST.SAUVEUR at 1500 and reopen at FLOBECQ at the same hour.

6. ACKNOWLEDGE.

Issued at 1830.   Lieut.Colonel, G.S.,
13th November 1918.   29th Division.

Distribution.

	Copy No.		Copy No.		Copy No.
G.O.C.	1	29th Bn.M.G.C.	24	Div.Recptn.Cmp.	34
G.S.	2-5	29 Div.Train.	25	French Mission.	35
"Q".	6-7	A.D.M.S.	26	Belgian Mission.	36
C.R.A.	8-14	D.A.D.V.S.	27	X Corps.	37-38
C.R.E.	15	D.A.P...	28	X Corps R.A.	39
Signals.	16	D.A.D.O.S.	29	X Corps H.A.	40
86th Inf.Bde.	17-18	Camp Cmdt.	30	30th Division.	41
87th Inf.Bde.	19-20	29 Div.M.T.Coy.	31	74th Division.	42
88th Inf.Bde.	21-22	29 Div.Emp.Coy.	32	S.A.A.Section.	43
1/2 Mon.R.(P)	23	Div.Gas Offr.	33	War Diary.	44-45

MARCH TABLE.

Serial No.	Date.	Unit.	From	To	Route	Remarks.
1	14th	87th Inf.Bde. Group.	ST. SAUVEUR area.	OGY-GHOY area.	F.15.Central - F.5.b.7.3. - X.30.a.6.0 - ELLEZELLES - FLOBECQ.	To pass X.30.a.6.0. at c900.
2	14th	1/2 .on R.(P).	ST. SAUVEUR area.	FLOBECQ.	As in Serial 1.	To pass X.30.a.6.0. at 1000 following 87th Inf.Bde.Group.
3	14th	15th Bde. R.H.A. V.Q. & No.1 Section D.A.C.	CELLES area.	WODECQ area.	D.24.Central - WATRIPONT - RENAIX - ELLEZELLES - T.25.d.6.0. - B.8.c.2.3.	To pass X.30.a.6.0. at 1030.
4	14th	88th Inf. Bde.Group.	ARC AINIERES area.	Area W. of FLOBECQ.	E.30.b.7.3. - F.25.a.8.5. - ST.SAUVEUR - F.16.Central - F.5.b.7.3. - X.30.a.6.0. - ELLEZELLES.	To pass X.30.a.6.0. at 1145.
5	14th	H.Q. and T Coy. 28th Bn. .G.C.	CELLES area.	FLOBECQ.	D.24.Central - WATRIPONT - RENAIX - ELLEZELLES.	To pass X.30.a.6.0. at 1700.
6	14th	497 Fd.Coy. R.E.	CELLES area.	MARAIS - A - L'EAU (E.21.)	- ditto -	To pass X.30.a.6.0. at 1510 to follow 29th Bn. G.Corps.
7	14th	S.A.A.Section.	-do-	WODECQ area.	As in Serial 3.	To pass X.30.a.6.0. at 1715, corps under orders of C.P.M. on arrival. Billeting parties to report WODECQ Church 1200.
8	15th	497 Fd.Coy.R.E.	MARAIS area.	LESSINES area.	FLOBECQ - OGY.	Time of start - Any. To come under orders of 88th Inf.Bde. on arrival.

Appendix 9

"C" FORM.
MESSAGES AND SIGNALS.
Army Form C. 2123.

Prefix .... Code 0750 Words 50
Received from 4BN By ....
Service Instructions ....

Sent, or sent out. At .... m.
To ....
By ....

Office Stamp: MGC 15.11.18

Handed in at 4B. Office 0750 m. Received 0755 m.

TO: 29 Bn M.G.C

Sender's Number.	Day of Month.	In reply to Number.	AAA
G.78	15	—	
The	29th	Bn.	M.G. Corps
will	concentrate	in	LESSINES
on	15th	under	orders
of	O.C.	Battalion,	and
the	completion	will	be
under	orders	of	O.C.
Battalion	and	Billets	from
88th	Bde	Acknowledge	
added	29 Bn	M.G. Corps	
Repld	all	concerned	

FROM: 29 Div
PLACE & TIME: 0700

MK 458   SECRET.

29th Bn. M.G. Corps Order No. 42.

Ref: Sheets 30 and 38.

1. The Battalion is concentrating in LESSINES today 15th Nov.

2. HQ, "A" Coy and Orr. Stores will march at 14.00 hours, forming up in order named on road running from T28 a 60.40 to T27b 40.10 facing S.W. with head of column at latter point. Ready to move at 14.00 hours.

3. Billetting parties from HQ, A Coy and Q.M. Stores will report to 2/Lt GADSBY at Bn. HQ at 10.30 hours. They will meet incoming Bn. at C.6.c.60.95.

4. ACKNOWLEDGE by bearer

Maurice ...
Capt.
for
LIEUT.-COLONEL,
COMDG. 19th BN. M.G. CORPS.

Copies: A Coy
Quartermaster and Sjts
(File)

SECRET.

49th Bn. M.G. Corps Order No 45.

Ref. Hub? Board 28.

1. The Bosh is concentrating in LECCINES today 15th inst.

2. HQ A Coy and Amm Stores will march at 14.00 hours forming up in order based on road running from T28.c.60.40 to T29.b.40.10, facing Ery with head of column at latter point. Ready to move at 14.00 hours.

3. Billetting parties from HQ A Coy
and Oms trans will report to
2/Lt Grocery at Bn HQ at
10.30 hours. They will make
morning Bn at C.16.c.60.95.

4. ACks by Bearer.

[signature]
Capt.
for
LIEUT-COLONEL
[stamp illegible]

Copies: A Coy
Oms and Sigs.
HQ

MK 456   SECRET

    OC, B Coy
        29th Bn MG Corps
    _____

1. In continuation of my MK 453 of today, your Company will move complete independently to billets in LESSINES.

2. You will move from present location at 4.00 hours and march by GHOY – Cqd 5.7 – C16c 40.95 – LESSINES.

3. Your Billeting party will report to 2/Lt GADSBY at 88th Bde HQ LESSINES at 11.30 hours.

4. Bn HQ, A and D Coys will march into LESSINES at about 15.30 hours.

5. Report location of new HQ to 2/Lt CROSBY.

6. ACKNOWLEDGE

Know one from
Capt.
for Lt Col. Comdg 29th Bn
MG Corps

16.11.18.

MK 456   SECRET

OC D Coy
29th Bn M.G. Corps.

1. The Bn. is concentrating in LESSINES today 13th inst.

2. Your Company will move forthwith independently from present location at 14.00 hours marching via B 8 c 25.30 – T 26 c 60.60 – FLOBECQ – OGY – LESSINES.

3. Billeting party will report to A.Q.M.G. Coy HQ at CHURCH FLOBECQ at 16.30 hours.

4. Report your new location to
Bn HQ in LESSINES as soon [as arrived?]

5. ACKNOWLEDGE

Lawrence Ross
Capt and Adjt
for Lt Col [Cooper?], 29th Bn MG Corps

15.11.18

SECRET.   Copy No. 24

29th DIVISION ORDER No. 290.

13th November 1918.

In continuation of 29th Division Warning Order No. O.G.S. 67/172 of 12th November,-

1. The following moves will take place to-day.-
   (a) The 88th Bde. (less troops on outpost) will concentrate in LESSINES.
   (b) 87th Bde. and Field Amb. will move to SAINT SAUVEUR area. Not to enter ARC ANWIERES before 1000.
   (c) 86th Bde. and Field Amb. to ARC ANWIERES and DAUREUX - not to enter CELLES before 1000 and to be clear of CELLES by 1200.
   (d) 17th Bde. R.F.A. and No. 2 Sec. D.A.C. to WODECQ. To be clear of ARC ANWIERES by 1000.
   (e) 15th, 96th F.A. Bdes, and H.Q. & No.1, Sec. D.A.C. to CELLES Not to pass HELCHIN CHURCH before 1100.
   (f) H.Q. and 1 Co. 29th Bn. M.G.C. to CELLES. Not to pass HELCHIN CHURCH before 1400.
   Billeting Officer to meet Staff Officer 29th Div. Art. at CELLES CHURCH at 1100.
   (g) S.A.A. Sec. to E.13. To clear HELCHIN CHURCH at 1000.

2. Supplies (including forage) for consumption on 14th will be delivered to units prior to marching off. If supplies are late, units must leave transport to bring them on. All supply vehicles proceeding east of the ESCAUT will be clear of HELCHIN Bridge by 0900.

3. Division Rear H.Q. will be established to-day at RENAIX.

4. ACKNOWLEDGE.

Issued at   OCUS
                                                    P.N. O'Connor
                                                    Lieut-Colonel
                                        General Staff, 29th Division.

Distribution.

	Copy No.		Copy No.
G.O.C.	1	D.A.D.O.S.	29
G.S.	2-5	Camp Comdt.	30
"Q"	6-7	29th Div. M.T. Co.	31
C.R.A.	8-14	226th Div. Emp. Co.	32
C.R.E.	15	Div. Gas Offr.	33
Signals.	16	Div. Reception Camp.	34
86th Inf. Bde.	17-18	French Mission.	35
87th Inf. Bde.	19-20	BELGIAN Mission.	36
88th Inf. Bde.	21-22	X Corps.	37-38
1/2 Monmouth R. (P)	23	-do- R.A.	39
29th Bn. M.G.C.	24	-do- D.A.	40
Div. Train.	25	30th Division.	41
A.D.M.S.	26	74th Division.	42
D.A.D.V.S.	27	War Diary.	43-44
D......	28	S.A.A.C.	45

S E C R E T.   Appendix 10   Copy No. 17

29th DIVISION ORDER NO. 293.

29th Div. H.Q.
16th November 1918.

Map reference, BELGIUM,
1/100,000. Sheets 5 & 6.

1. In accordance with the terms of Armistice, the occupied portions of France, Belgium and Luxembourg are to be evacuated by the enemy by November 26th.

   A further withdrawal East of the Rhine will take place at a later date.

2. The IInd Corps will advance in the order:-

   29th Division. Right.)
   41st Division. Left.) 1st Echelon.

   34th Division. Right.)
   9th Division. Left.   ) 2nd Echelon.

   Corps Artillery.   3rd Echelon.

   A Canadian Division will be advancing on right of 29th Division.

3. The advance will be covered by the cavalry advancing one day's march ahead.

4. The 29th Division will march on the 18th November to the line:-
   Road through SOIGNES and ENGHIEN between HORRUES (exclusive) and point   where railway crosses Road one mile N.N.W. of ENGHIEN.

   A halt for two days, will be made on the above line and in the area West of it.

5. (a) The march will be carried out in accordance with attached March Table in four Brigade Groups (see Appendix "A"):-
   87th Inf.Bde. (Right) and 88th Inf.Bde. Groups leading.
   86th Inf.Bde. (Right) and R.A.Groups in rear.

   (b) On reaching the line in para 4, the dividing line between leading brigades will be an E. and W. line through MAIREBOIS.

   (c) The march will be completed by 1300.

6. Throughout the advance to the Rhine, all military precautions against surprise will be taken, in accordance with 29th Division Instruction No.1 of this date.

7. (a) D.H.Q. will close at FLOBECQ on 18th instant at 0900.

   (b) During the march the Divisional Headquarters Report Centre will be at the rear end of the 88th Inf.Bde. Group.

   (c) D.H.Q. will open at ENGHIEN at 1400.

8. ACKNOWLEDGE.

Issued at 8.50 p.m.

Lieut.Colonel, G.S.,
29th Division.

P.T.O

DISTRIBUTION.

G.O.C.	1
G.S.	2-3
"Q".	4-5
C.R.A.	6-7
C.R.E.	8
Signals.	9
86th Inf.Bde.	10-11
87th Inf.Bde.	12-13
88th Inf.Bde.	14-15
1/2nd Mon.R.(P).	16
29th Bn.M.G.Corps.	17
Div.Train.	18
A.D.M.S.	19
D.A.D.V.S.	20
D.A.P.M.	21
D.A.D.O.S.	22
Camp Comdt.	23
29th Div.M.T.Coy.	24
Div.Recptn.Camp.	25
Belgian Mission.	26
II Corps.	27-28
41st Division.	29
34th Division.	30
War Diary.	31-32.

SECRET

29th Bn. M.G. Corps Order No 41

Ref. Sheets 29, 30, 37 and 38.

1. The following moves will take place on the 14th inst:

   Bn. HQ and A Coy will move to FLOBECQ (Sheet 30).

   D Coy will move into 86th Bde group in area W. of ELLEZELLES (Sheet 30)

2. The above will move as one column forming up on road running from D24c5.0 – D24b4.0 facing NE in order Bn. HQ, A Coy, HQ. transport, D Coy.

II

Head of column to be at road junction
D24 d 2.8. Ready to move 09.30 hrs.
(Column passes X30 a 6.0 at 13.00 hrs)

3. Route will be: D24 – WATRIPONT –
RENAIX – ELLEZELLES – FLOBECQUE.
D Coy will have its column W. of
ELLEZELLES at point where its guide
meets it moving to billets in 56th
Bde area.

4. Billeting parties proceed as follows:—
(a) Bn. HQ and A Coy report to 2/Lt.
GADSBY at road junction D24 d 2.8
at 09.00 hours and proceed to
FLOBECQ. Meet incoming Bn. at
30/T 76 d 50.55.

II

4. D Coy billeting party report to
Billeting Officer 80½ Bde at
11.00 hours.
T26 c 7.6 (Sheet 30) at [illegible] KORTA

5. A haversack ration will be
carried — Dinners on arrival in
new area.

6. Bn HQ closes at present location
at 09.00 hrs and reopens at
FLOBECQ on arrival.

7. Sick parade — 07.00 hrs at
Bn HQ

8. ACKNOWLEDGE

Ammunition Coy

Copies: A Coy   p. Lt. Col. GUISE, OC 9 Bn M.G.
D Coy
QM and Sigs.   Issued at hrs

SECRET.

29th Bn. MACHINE GUN CORPS Operation Order No. 40.
━━

Ref. sheets 29 and 37 1:40,000.

1. The Battalion (less "B" and "C" Companies) will move to CELLES today the 13th inst.

2. H.Q. "D" and "A" Companies and H.Q. Transport will form up in the order named in column of route on the ST.GENOIS - HELCHIN road facing S.E. with the head of the column at railway crossing at U.16.d.05.30. Column to be ready to move at 13.45 hours.

3. Dinners will be at 12.15 hours.

4. Dress - full marching order. Blankets will be carried on limbers.

5. The usual billetting parties for H.Q. Companies and Q.M.Stores will report to 2/Lt. GADSBY at H.Q. Mess at 09.30 hours. They will meet a Staff Officer 29th Divisional R.A. at CELLES Church at 11.00 hours to arrange billets. They will meet the incoming battalion at D.16.a.95.60. Probable time of arrival 16.00 hours.

6. Bn. H.Q. closes at present location at 12.45 hours and reopens on arrival at CELLES.

7. ACKNOWLEDGE.

13th November 1918.

                                              Lieut.Colonel,
                              Commanding 29th Bn. M.G.Corps.

Copies to :

    "A" Coy.
    "D" "
    "B" ") For information.
    "C" ")
    Q.M.
    Signals Officer.
    29th Division "G"
    29th Division "A"
    File (2)

SECRET.   Appendix II.
                                              Copy No. 9

29th BN. M.G.CORPS.

Operation Order No. 43

Reference: 1:100,000 TOURNAI (5) and BRUSSELS (6).
           1:40,000 Sheet 38.

1. The Battalion will march East with 88th Brigade Group tomorrow 18th inst. to area MAIRELOIS - HOVES - ENGHIEN - MARCQ - ST.PIERRE CAPELLE, marching via BOIS DE LESSINES and BASSILLY. Length of march about 10 miles (dependent on exact billetting area of Battn.)

2. The Brigade Group will be covered by an Advanced Guard of one infantry Battn. to which will be attached two Sections of Machine Guns. These will be found by "C" Coy., and will be under the command of 2/Lieut. G.E.ROLPH (M.C.), who will report to O.C. 4th WORCESTER REGT. and come under his orders for the march.

3. The Battn. (less two Sections of "C" Coy.) will form up as follows:-

    Battn.H.Q. and H.Q.transport in road outside Battn.Orderly Room.

    "C" Coy. (less two Sections) in street leading to Coy. billets with head of Coy. resting on main road at C.17.c.15.65.

    "A" Coy. in road running from C.23.a.60.95 - C.17.c.45.30. with head of column resting on main road at C.17.c.60.35.

    "B" Coy. in road running from C.23.a.60.95 - C.17.c.60.35. with head of column at latter point.

    "D" Coy. in street running from Church in C.23.b.05.80 - C.17.d.05.80.

    When the Battn. moves to the starting point at C.17.d.20.10. "C" Coy. will join column behind Battn.H.Q. followed by "A" Coy., "B" Coy. and "D" Coy. as column passes them. (H.Q. transport will march in rear of the whole column).
    H.Q. and Companies must be ready to move at 08:50 hours.
    Head of Battn. passes starting point at 09:00 hours.
    Distances between Coys. will be only 10 yards.

4. Dress - Full marching order with caps. Greatcoats will be carried in packs, Jerkins on limbers. (Drivers will wear greatcoats and jerkins).

5. Blankets will be carried by lorry. They will be stacked by Coys. at Q.M. Stores by 07:30 hours, rolled in bundles of 10 (not by teams or Sections).

6. Breakfasts will be at 06:45 hours.
   Dinners on arrival (i.e. at about 13.15 hours.)

7. Sick parades for all coys. will be at the Regtl. Aid Post at 07:15 hours.

8. Instructions regarding billetting parties will be issued later. The usual parties from Coys. and H.Q. will hold themselves in readiness to proceed in advance very early tomorrow 18th inst.

9. ACKNOWLEDGE.

                                    [signature] Capt.
                                    for Lieut. Colonel,
                                    Comdg. 29th Bn. M.G.Corps.

17th November 1918.

                                                     P.T.O.

APPENDIX "A" to 29th DIVISION ORDER No.293.

Composition of Brigade Groups for 18th instant.

86th Inf. Brigade Group.   86th Inf. Brigade.

                                                             1/2 Monmouth Regt. (P).
                                                             510th Field Coy. R.E.
                                                             No.2 Coy. Div. Train.
                                                             89th Field Ambulance.

87th Inf. Brigade Group.   87th Inf. Brigade.

                                                             455th Field Coy. R.E.
                                                             No.3 Coy. Div. Train.
                                                             87th Field Ambulance.

88th Inf. Brigade Group.   88th Inf. Brigade.

                                                             497th Field Coy. R.E.
                                                             29th Battn. M.G.Corps.
                                                             No.4 Coy. Div. Train.
                                                             88th Field Ambulance.

R.Artillery Group.   15th Brigade R.H.A.
                                                             17th Brigade R.F.A.
                                                             38th A.F.A. Brigade.
                                                             29th D.A.C.
                                                             No.1 Coy. Div. Train.

-o-o-o-o-o-o-o-o-o-o-o-

M A R C H   T A B L E (To accompany 29th Div. Order No.295).

Serial No.	Date.	Unit.	From	To Billeting area.	Route.	Remarks.
1	Nov.18th.	87th Bde. Group.	WANNEBECQ area.	Boundary. HORRUES (excl) HAIREBOIS (excl) N of latter to S of BOIS DE CAMERON thence S.E. to MASY thence to HORRUES (excl).	GHISLENGHIEN THENCE ANY south of dividing line and North of line through HORRUES.	Clear N. and S. line through WANNEBECQ by 0930.
2	do	88th Bde Group.	LESSINES area.	HAIREBOIS - HOVES ENGHIEN-MARCQ - ST PIERRE CAPELLE.	BOIS de LESSINES - BASSILLY. HILTS or ENGHIEN - also B. de LESSINES-ST.P. CAPELLE, south of BIEVENE.	Clear LESSINES by 0930.
3	do	86th Bde. Group.	FLOBECQ area.	GIBECQ - SILLY. BASILLY - GHISLE- -NGHIEN-MELLEDECQ.	LAHAMAIDE - WANNEBECQ - MELLEBECQ or CHISLENGHIEN.	(Bridges exist at LOCK and IRON Bridge). Road. LA CAVES - BASSILLY STN - INN at K.S. 38 not available.
4	do	R.A. Group.	WODECQ area.	CULOT DU BOIS LA ELIA - CROISETTE MARIANG - PIBROEK - ROMPONT - LA CAVES HULD - BOIS DE LESS- -INES-EN HAUT-OLLIG- -NIES, east of main road.	LESSINES - BOIS DE LESSINES, thence as for Serial No.2, or BASSILLY STN INN.K.S.38.	
5	do	D.H.Q.	FLOBECQ.	ENGHIEN	(As for Serial No.2.)	arch in front of Serial 4 - clear road junction K.S.48 by 0830.

NOTE. K.S. = Kilometre stone.

Appendix 12

SECRET.
COPY NO. 10.

88th Infantry Brigade Order No. 230.

Reference BRUSSELS 1/100,000.   20th November, 1918.

1. The 29th Division is continuing the march towards the frontier on the 21st, 22nd, 23rd, and 24th November. It will halt on the 25th and 26th.
On the left the 9th Division is today relieving the 41st Division.

2. The 88th Inf. Bde. Group will march on the 21st November, in accordance with the accompanying March Table, to billets in BRAME LE CHATEAU area.

ADVD. GD.
1 pltn Y.Dns.(Cycling)
13 Bty R.F.A.
1 sec R.E.
2/Hamps.R.
2 secs M.Gs.
1 Coy. Pioneers.

3. Advanced Guard, as per margin, will be under the command of Lieut-Colonel H.C.WESTMORLAND, D.S.O. Instructions will be issued separately.
An officer from each Unit in the Advanced Guard will report to Lieut-Colonel H.C.WESTMORLAND, D.S.O. at H.Q. 2nd Hampshire Regt, 4.A.45.34, at 1700 today, 20th November.

4. On arrival in Billeting area O.C. Advanced Guard will arrange to picket all main roads crossing the BRAME LE CHATEAU - HAL Road from the direction of the enemy, from BRAME LE CHATEAU to HAL exclusive. Further instructions will be issued verbally.

5. Arrangements will regard to Halts, Transport, Stragglers, Orderlies reporting to Brigade H.Q. at the conclusion of the march, will be as in Brigade Order No. 229. These arrangements will stand for all marches until further orders are issued.

6. Units will report arrival in billets to Brigade H.Q.

7. Brigade H.Q. will close at ENGHIEN at 0900 and will march at the Head of the Main Body. Brigade H.Q. in Billeting Area will be opened in BRAME LE CHATEAU; exact location will be notified later.

8. ACKNOWLEDGE.

                                   Captain,
Issued at 1300.   Brigade Major, 88th Infantry Bde.

Copies to 1 - 4 Staff.
5 4th Worcestershire Regt.
6 2nd Hampshire Regt.
7 2nd Leinster Regt.
8 88th Trench Mortar Battery.
9 497th Fd. Coy, R.E.
10 29th Bn. M.G.Corps.
11 88th Fd. Amb.Co.
12 No. 4 Coy, Train.
13 13th Bty R.F.A.
14 Detachment Yorkshire Dragoons. (Cyclists)
15 86th Inf. Bde.
16 87th Inf. Bde.
17 Bde on Left, 9th Div.
18 29th Div. "G".
19 D.A.P.M.
20 S.S.O. 29th Div.
21 File.
22 Diary.

SECRET. Appendix 13 COPY NO. _____

29th BATTN. M.G. CORPS.

Operation Order No. 45.

Reference Map: BRUSSELS 6, 1/100,000.

1. The Battalion (less "C" Company) will march with 88th Brigade Group tomorrow, 23rd inst., to billets in the vicinity of OHAIN.
Length of march - about 9½ miles.

2. Two Sections of "B" Company will be detailed as part of the Advanced Guard to the Brigade. They will be under command of Capt. L.K. MORRIS, and will come under the orders of O.C., 2nd LEINSTER REGT. for the march.

3. The Battalion will form up ready to move at 09.00 hours on road running 4.D.01.18 to 4.D.12.18, facing East, head of column at Bridge 4.D.12.18.
Order of march will be - Personnel of Bn.H.Q., "A", "B", and "D" Coys., Transport of "A", "B", and "D" Coys. and H.Q.

4. Dress - full marching order. Greatcoats will be carried in packs, jerkins on limbers and blankets on lorries.

5. All blankets will be at Q.M.Stores, rolled in bundles of 10, by 07.30 hours.

6. Breakfasts: 06.45 hours.
Dinners: On arrival (i.e., about 13.00 hours).
Sick parades for all Coys: 07.00 hours.

7. Usual billetting parties will meet 2/Lieut.A.F.GADSBY at 07.15 hours at Bn. H.Q.Mess
One guide per Company will meet Battalion at Cross Roads 4.F.23.16.

8. ACKNOWLEDGE.

22nd November 1918.

A.F.Gadsby 2/Lt
for Lieut.Colonel,
Comdg 29th Bn. M.G.Corps.

Copies to:
1. "A" Coy.
2. "B" Coy.
3. "D" Coy.
4. Q.M. and Signals Officer.
5. R.S.M.
6. "C" Coy.) for information.
7. 88th Inf.Bde.)
8 & 9. File.
10 & 11. War Diary.

SECRET.   Copy No. _____

29th BN. M.G. CORPS.
Operation Order No. 44.

Reference: 1:100,000 BRUSSELS 6.

1. The Battalion (less "C" Coy.) will march with 88th Brigade Group tomorrow, 21st inst., to the BRAME-LE-CHATEAU area, via SAINTES and TUBIZE.
    Length of march – about 12 miles. The Divisional Band will march with the Battalion.

2. Two Sections of "A" Coy. will be detailed as part of the Advanced Guard to the Brigade. They will be under command of Capt.V.J.H.BRINT, and will come under the orders of O.C. 2nd HAMPSHIRE REGT. for the march.

3. The Battalion will not march in the usual M.G.Battalion formation. Battalion H.Q., "A" Coy. (less two Sections), "B" Coy. and "D" Coy. (companies without transport) will form up in order named on main ATH - ENGHIEN road facing East with head of column at gate leading to Battalion Orderly Room.
    Transport will follow on bloc in order "A", "B", "D", H.Q. Column will be ready to move at 09.30 hours.

4. As the Battalion moves off from each halt, the leading company will remain at the side of the road, so as to allow the second company to come to the head of the column.

5. Dress – Full marching order. Greatcoats will be carried in packs, jerkins on limbers and blankets on lorries.

6. All blankets will be at Q.M.Stores, rolled in bundles of 10, by 08.15 hours.

7. Breakfasts: 07.45 hours.
   Dinners: On arrival (i.e., about 14.30 hours.)
   Sick parades for all companies: 07.00 hours.

8. Instructions regarding billetting parties will be issued later.

9. ACKNOWLEDGE.

20th November 1918.
                                            Lieut.Colonel,
                                    Comdg 29th Bn. M.G.Corps.

Copies to : 1. "A" Coy.
             2. "B" "
             3. "D" "
             4. Quartermaster.
             5. Signals Officer.
             6. 88th Bde (for information).
             7.) War Diary.
             8.)
             9.) File.
            10.)

MARCH TABLE issued with 88th Infantry Brigade Order No. 230.

Serial No.	"A" Unit.	"B" Starting Point.	"C" Time.	"D" To Billeting Area.	"E" Route.
1.	88th bde H.Q. & T.M.B.	Road Junction 4.A.52.40.35.	0930	BRAME LE CHATEAU	4.A.52.40.35. -
2.	2nd Leinster Regt.	do.	0933	do.	SAINTES -
3.	4th Worcestershire Regt.	do.	0940	do.	4.J.17.57. -
4.	29th M.G. Battn.	do.	0947	do.	TUBIZE -
5.	497th Fd. Coy, R.E.	do.	1007	do.	BRAME LE CHATEAU.
6.	88th Fd. Ambce.	do.	1010	do.	do.
7.	No. A Coy, Train.	do.	1013	do.	do.

26/11/18.

F.S. Williams,
Captain,
Brigade Major, 88th Infantry Brigade.

Appendix 14

SECRET.
COPY NO. 10

88th Infantry Brigade Order No. 232.

Reference BRUSSELS 1/100,000. 24th November, 1918.

1. The 88th Infantry Brigade Group will march to the OTTIGNIES Area tomorrow, 25th November, in accordance with the accompanying March Table.

2. Units will report arrival in billets to Brigade Report Centre which will be opened at OTTIGNIES Church. Location of Brigade H.Q. will be notified later.

3. Brigade H.Q. will close at CHATEAU, ST LAMBERT, 1000 and will march at the Head of the Column.

4. ACKNOWLEDGE.

J. Stokins
Captain,
Brigade Major, 88th Infantry Brigade.

Issued at 1845.

Copies to 1 - 4 Staff.
5 4th Worcestershire Regt.
6 2nd Hampshire Regt.
7 2nd Leinster Regt.
8 88th Trench Mortar Battery.
9 497th Field Coy, R.E.
10 29th M.G.Battn.
11 88th Fd. Amboe.
12 No. 4 Coy, Train.
13 13th Bty, R.F.A.
14 "B" Coy, 1/2nd Monmouth Regt.
15 Detachment Yorkshire Dragoons (Cyclists).
16 86th Inf. Bde.
17 87th Inf. Bde.
18 D.A.P.M.
19 29th Div. "G".
20 S.S.O.
21 File.
22 Diary.

MARCH TABLE issued with 88th Infantry Brigade Order No. 232.

Serial No.	"A" Unit.	"B" Starting Point.	"C" Time.	"D" To Billeting Area	"E" Route
1.	Bde H.Q., F.M.B. & Pltn v.Dns.	Road Junction A.G.09.10.	1030	OTTIGNIES Area.	Road Junction 4.G.09.10. Cross Roads 5.G.12.92. CEROUX MOUSTY Road Junction 5.G.75.92. OTTIGNIES.
2.	4th Worcester Regt.	do.	1033	do.	
3.	2nd Hampshire Regt.	do.	1040	do.	
4.	"3" Coy. 1/2nd Mons.	do.	1047	do.	
5.	2nd Leinster Regt.	3 Road Junction 9.F.80.23	1040	do.	
6.	24th M.G.Battn.	do.	1050	do.	
7.	13th Bty. R.F.A.	do.	1115	do.	
8.	497th Field Coy.	do.	1120	do.	
9.	88th Fd. Ambce.	do.	1125	do.	
10.	No. 4 Coy. Train.	do.	1130	do.	

24/11/1918.

Captain,
Brigade Major, 88th Infantry Brigade.

MARCH TABLE
to accompany 88th Infantry Brigade Order No. 231.

Serial No.	"A" Unit.	"B" Starting Point.	"C" Time.	"D" To Billeting Area.	"E" Route.
1.	88th Bde H.Q. & T.M.B.	Cross Roads 4.D.58.21.	0930	ST LAMBERT	Cross Roads 4.D.58.21. — Cross Roads 4.E.36.40. —
2.	4th Worcestershire R.	do.	0933	do.	
3.	2nd Hampshire Regt.	do.	0940	do.	Road Fork 4.E.46.22. — Bifurcation 4.E.62.24. —
4.	29th M.G.Battn.	do.	0947	OHAIN	Cross Roads 4.E.94.17 —
5.	497th Field Coy.R.E.	do.	1007	ST LAMBERT	Farm 4.F.23.16 —
6.	88th Field Ambce.	do.	1010	do.	Cross Roads 4.F.26.13 —
7.	No. 4 Coy. Train.	do.	1013	do.	Cross Roads 4.F.61.05 — ST LAMBERT.

F.H.Barnard
Captain,
for Brigade Major, 88th Infantry Brigade.

22/11/18.

SECRET

Copy No. 10

*** 88th INFANTRY BRIGADE ORDER No. 231 ***

22nd November, 1918.

Reference BRUSSELS 1/100,000.

1. The 29th Division is continuing the march towards the frontier on the 23＊24 November.

2. The 88th Infantry Brigade Group will march on 23rd November, in accordance with accompanying March Table, to billets in the OHAIN - ST. LAMBERT Area.

ADVD.
GD.
1 pltn
Y.Dns.
(Cyclists)
13 Bty.
R.F.A.
1 Sec. R.E.
2/Leins.R.
2 Secs
M.G's.
1 Coy.
Pioneers.

3. Advanced Guard as per margin will be under the command of Lieut-Colonel H.W.WELDON, D.S.O. Instructions will be issued separately.

An Officer from each Unit in the Advanced Guard will report to Lieut-Colonel H.W.WELDON, D.S.O., at Headquarters 2nd Leinster Regt. at 1700 today.

4. On arrival in billeting area O.C. Advanced Guard will arrange to picket the ST. LAMBERT - RIXENSART Road and the ST. LAMBERT - CEROUX-MOUSTY Road. Further instructions will be issued verbally.

5. Units will report arrival in billets to Brigade Headquarters.

6. Brigade Headquarters will close at BRAINE LE CHATEAU at 0900 and will march at the head of the main body.
Brigade Headquarters in new billeting area will be opened in the Chateau, 4.F.89.24. on arrival.

7. ACKNOWLEDGE.

F H Harrod
Captain,

Issued through
Signals at 1430

for
Brigade Major, 88th Infantry Brigade.

D I S T R I B U T I O N :-

Copy. No. 1 - 4. Staff.
5. 4th Worcestershire Regt.
6. 2nd Hampshire Regt.
7. 2nd Leinster Regt.
8. 88th Trench Mortar Battery.
9. 497th Field Coy. R.E.
10. 29th Battn. M.G.C.
11. 88th Field Ambulance.
12. No. 4 Coy. Train A.S.C.
13. 13th Battery R.F.A.
14. Detachment Yorkshire Dragoons (Cyclists)
15. 86th Infantry Brigade.
16. 87th " "
17. "E" Coy. 1/2nd Monmouth Regt. (Pioneers).
18. Right Brigade, 9th Division.
19. 29th Division "G".
20. D.A.P.M., 29th Division.
21. S.S.O., 29th Division.
22. File.
23. Diary.

Appendix 15

SECRET.
COPY NO....

88th Infantry Brigade Order No. 233.

Reference: BRUSSELS 1/100,000.   25th November, 1918.

1. The 29th Division will halt tomorrow, 26th November.

2. The following re-organisation of groups will take place:-

    13th Bty R.F.A.
    29th M.G.Battn (less 1 Coy).
    "B" Coy, 1/2nd Monmouthshire Regt

    will join the 86th Infantry Brigade Group, and will march tomorrow, 26th November, in accordance with the accompanying March Table.

3. Billeting areas are allotted as under:-

    13th Bty R.F.A.   )
    29th M.G.Battn (less 1 Coy)   ) - CORBAIS.
    "B" Coy, 1/2nd Monmouth Regt. - LIBERSART (N. of TOURINNES ST LAMBERT)

    Billeting parties will arrive there at 1000.

4. The above Units will notify 86th Inf. Bde. H.Q. on their arrival in billets.

5. 86th Inf. Bde. H.Q. will be at NIL ST VINCENT.

6. ACKNOWLEDGE.

                                        Captain,
Issued at _____   Brigade Major, 88th Infantry Brigade.

Copies to 1 "A" Staff.
           5 4th Worcestershire Regt.
           6 2nd Hampshire Regt.
           7 2nd Leinster Regt.
           8 88th Trench Mortar Bty.
           9 497th Fd. Coy, R.E.
          10 29th M.G. Battn.
          11 88th Fd. Ambce.
          12 No. 4 Coy, A.S.C.
          13 13th Bty R.F.A.
          14 "B" Coy, 1/2nd Monmouth Regt
          15 86th Inf. Bde.
          16 87th Inf. Bde.
          17 29th Division "G".
          18 S.S.C.
          19 D.A.P.M.
          20 File.
          21 Diary.

*** MARCH TABLE ***

to accompany 88th Infantry Brigade Order No. 233 of 25th Novr., 1918.

Serial No.	"A" UNIT	"B" Starting Point	"C" Time	"D" To	"E" Route
1.	15th Battery R.F.A.	Road Junction 5.G.74.92.	1000	CORBAIS	5.G.74.92. – 5.H.32.61. – 5.H.74.74.
2.	29th Battalion M.G.C.	– ditto –	1015	CORBAIS	
3.	"B" Coy., 1/2nd Monmouth Regt.	– ditto –	0930	LIBERSART North & TOURINNES ST LAMBERT	– ditto –

F. Stevenson
Captain,
Brigade Major, 88th Infantry Brigade.

25th November, 1918.

SECRET.

29th Bn. M.G. Corps.

Move Orders for November 25th 1918.

Ref: Sheet 6 BRUSSELS 1:100,000.

Destination: OTTIGNIES

Route and length of March: RENIVAL – CATURIAUX – CEROUX – MOUSTY. About 7 miles.

Forming up place and order of march:
Form up in order HQ, A, B, D, Coys, followed by all Transport as on last march, on road running from Cross Roads, 4.F.61.43. – 4.F.80.23. facing S.E. Head of Column at road junction 4.F.76.33

Ready to move at 10.25 hours.

Orders for Billetting parties:
Report 2/Lt GATSBY at Orderly Room at 07.15 hours. (usual parties)

ACKNOWLEDGE.

Lieut. Col.,
Cmdg. 29th Bn. M.G. Corps.

24th Nov. 1918.

Copies to: A
            B } Coys
            D
            Adv. and Signals Officer
            File & Diary

P.T.O.

Ref. Reverse:

1. All Blankets will be stacked at Qtr. Stores in bundles of 10 by 09.00 hours.

2. The Band will march the Battn. as far as the starting point and will then fall out and join the R.E. Field Coy.

CAPT. & ADJT.
29th BN. M. G. CORPS.

SECRET   Copy No. 10

86th INFANTRY BRIGADE ORDER No. 297.

Ref Map - BRUSSELS 1/100,000.   26th November 1918.

1. **INFORMATION.**
   (a) The Division is continuing the advance on Nov. 27th and 28th on a one Brigade Front.
   (b) The 86th Infantry Brigade Group will be in Support.
   (c) On Nov. 26th, the undermentioned Units will join the Brigade Group and be accommodated as shewn:-
   13th Battery R.F.A.   CORBAIS.
   29th Bn M.G.C. (less 1 Coy)   CORBAIS.
   B Coy 1/2 Mons Regt   LILERSART.
   (d) On arrival at Starting Point, B Coy 1/2 Mons Regt will on Nov.27 come under orders of O.C. 1/Lancs. Fus until further orders.

2. **INTENTION.**
   On Nov. 27th the 86th Brigade Group will move to billets in the HANRET Area. Moves will be in accordance with Table attached.

3. **ADVANCE GUARD.**
   The 2/Royal Fusiliers will detail an advance guard - strength one Coy. to be in position by 10.45.
   One section of cyclists will report to O.C. Advance Guard at Starting Point at 10.30.

4. **RECONNAISSANCE.**
   Os. C. Units will reconnoitre roads to S.P. so as to ensure that columns arrive at the S.P. at the correct time.

5. **TRANSPORT.**
   (a) Lewis Gun limbers and pack animals will follow each Coy.
   (b) 1st and 2nd line transport behind Units must be kept closed up so as to prevent loss of distance on the march.

6. **TRAFFIC.**
   (a) Care must be taken that halted transport does not block roads which may be used by Units moving to S.P.
   (b) Motor Ambulances are not to interfere with Units moving to SP

7. **BILLETING.**
   Billeting Parties will proceed independently. Billeting Party of B Coy. 1/2 Mons Regt will report to O.i/c Billeting Party 1/Lancs. Fus. at the CHURCH, HANRET.

8. **REPORTS.**
   Locations and marching-in states to be sent to Brigade Headquarters HARLUE by 18.00.

9. ACKNOWLEDGE

Issued at 15.30 p.m.

G. Heffernan
Major,
A/Brigade Major,
86th Inf. Brigade.

SECRET.

29th BATTALION MACHINE GUN CORPS.

Move orders for 28th November 1918.

Ref: Sheet 6 BRUSSELS, 1:100,000.

Destination: CORBAIS.
Route and length of march: MOUSTY — COURT ST. ETIENNE — MONT ST. GUIBERT.
~~MOUSTIES — LA BARAQUE~~
About 9 miles.

Forming up place and order of march: On main road through
    village, with head of column at road junction immediately
    south of R in CORBAIS facing EAST.   Order, H.Q., "A",
    "B", "C" Coys. - Transport in rear.

Ready to move at 09.00 hours. 09.35

Orders for billetting parties: Report to 2/Lieut. GATSBY at
    Church at 08.30 hours.

ACKNOWLEDGE.

                                Lieut.Colonel,
                                Comdg. 29th Bn. M.G.Corps.

28th November 1918.

        Copies to : "A", "B", "C" Coys.
                     Q.M. and Signals Officer.
                     File and Diary.

1.   No Company is to fall in for the move before 08.40 hours.
     In the past men have been kept waiting with packs on much too
     long.   The same applies to limbers, which will not be loaded
     up an hour before moving off and left with all the weight on
     the animals' shoulders.

2.   Blankets to be at Q.M.Stores by 08.00 hours.

3.   Sick parades: 07.15 hours.

28th November 1918.   Capt.& Adjt.,
                                          29th Bn. M.G.Corps.

WARNING ORDER

88 Bde no B4/290

29th M.G. Battn
13th Bty R.F.A.
'B' Coy 2nd Hants

Tomorrow, 26th November, the following unit will be transferred to 86th Inf Bde:-

13th Bty R.F.A.
29th M.G. Bn } to CORBAIS
(less 1 Coy)

'B' Coy 2nd Hants } to NIL ST VINCENT

Billetting parties should arrive at the above mentioned places at 1000.

86th Inf Bde H.Q. moves today to NIL ST VINCENT.

F. S. Whinney
Captain
25-11-18 Bde Major 88 Inf Bde

MESSAGES AND SIGNALS.
Army Form C. 2121.
(In pads of 100.)

Prefix......Code......m	Words.	Charge.	This message is on a/c of:	Recd. at......m
Office of Origin and Service Instructions.	Sent			Date..........
	At.......m.		............Service.	From........
	To......			
	By......		(Signature of "Franking Officer.")	By........

TO { A B D } Coys QM RSM

Sender's Number.	Day of Month.	In reply to Number.	
BK 762	26th	→	AAA

Reference move order for 27th
aaa Column will be ready
to move at 08.30 hours
and not as stated aaa Sick
parade 06.45 hours aaa
Billeting parties 08.00 hours
aaa ACKNOWLEDGE by bearer

From 29th Bn. M.G. Corps
Place
Time
The above may be forwarded as now corrected. (Z) [signature] Capt
                                                    Censor.   Signature of Addressor or person authorised to telegraph in his name.

※ This line should be erased if not required.
(3198.) Wt. W 12952/M 1294. 375,000 Pads. 1/17. H.W. & V., Ld. (E. 818.)

S E C R E T.

29th BATTALION MACHINE GUN CORPS.

Move Orders for 27th November 1918.

Ref: Sheet 6 BRUSSELS, 1:100,000.

Destination: LONGCHAMPS in G. K.

Route and length of march: NIL ABBESSE - NIL ST.VINCENT - ORBAIS - PERWEZ - AISNE EN REFAIL - MEHAIGNE.
About 14½ miles.

Forming up place and order of march: WAVRE-GISTOUX main road facing S.E. Head of column at Battn.Orderly Room. Order H.Q., "A", "B", "D" Coys. (Transport in rear).
"D" Coy. can form up in road leading on to main road.

Ready to move at 09.00 hours.

Orders for billeting parties: Report to 2/Lieut. GADSBY at Orderly Room at 08.30 hours.

ACKNOWLEDGE.

                                                          [signature] Capt

26th November 1918.
                                                        Lieut-Colonel,
                                                        Comdg. 29th Bn. M.G.Corps.

Copies to: "A", "B", "D" Coys.
            Q.M. AND Signals Officer.
            File and Diary.

There will be a halt for dinners, (probably between PERWEZ and AISCHE EN REFAIL) at midday.
Sick parade: 07.15 hours.
Blankets to be at Q.M.Stores by 08.00 hours.

                                                      [signature]
                                                      Capt.& Adjt.,
                                                       29th Bn. M.G.Corps.

MESSAGES AND SIGNALS.

TO Units of 86 Group

Sender's Number: H24
Day of Month: 24

Billeting areas issued tomorrow
LANC FUS)
2 MGC) ANTHEIT
6 RE)
8 ...)
B de Hq) WANZE
2 Roy Irish) WANZE
1 RDF MOHA
13 Bty RFA LAHESBAYE

Parties [in] ANTHEIT to meet S Capt
on main Rd at [in] LAHESBAYE
at 1030 Ack by scary
Acknowledge on envelope

From 86 Bde

MESSAGES A[ND]

Prefix......Code......m	Words.	Charge.	This message is on a/c of :	Recd. at ....m
Office of Origin and Service Instructions.	Sent		..................Service.	Date............
	At.........m.			From............
	To........			
	By........		(Signature of "Franking Officer.")	By............

TO { A B C D } Coys. OM. RSM

Sender's Number.	Day of Month.	In reply to Number.	AAA
BK 765	27th	—	

Reference tomorrow's move aaa
Battalion will billet in ANTHEIT
not as stated aaa Distance
about 18 miles aaa Duncan
known as Same Scafor
"Cat" Billeting parties report
07.30 hours near Duncan
starting from roads

From: Sgt Bn HQ Comd
Place:
Time:

The above may be forwarded as now corrected. (Z) Franking Officer.

SECRET.

29th Bn. M.G. Corps.

Move Orders for Nov. 28th 1918.

Ref: Sheet 6 BRUSSELS and Sheet 7 LIEGE 1:100,000

Destination: HERON

Route and length of March: L'ANGLE – FORVILLE – BIERWART. About 11 miles.

Forming up place and order of march:
In village street facing E, with head of column at CHURCH – Order BHQ. A, B, D Coys. Transport in rear.

Ready to move at 09.15 hours.

Orders for Billeting parties:
Report to Capt. GADSBY at CHURCH at 08.00 hours.

ACKNOWLEDGE.

Lieut. Col.,
Cmdg. 29th Bn. M.G. Corps.

27 – 11 – 1918.

Copies to: A, B and D Coys. QM and Sig. Officer
File

1. Blankets at QM Stores by 08.15 hours.
2. Sick Parade at 07.30 hours.

29 Bn MG Corps
Vol 10
November 1916
December

On His Majesty's Service.

D.A.G. J.H.Q. 3rd Echelon

A.D.M.S.,
61st
(HIGHLAND DIVISION).
No. .... W.D.#
Date ....

WAR DIARY
INTELLIGENCE SUMMARY

War Diary 1st - 31st Dec'r 1918.
29th Bn. Machine Gun Corps.

WAR DIARY
INTELLIGENCE SUMMARY

(Erase heading not required.)

Army Form C. 2118.

Place	Date	Hour	Summary of Events and Information	Remarks and references to Appendices
REMOUCHAMPS (Sheet MARCHE 9) I.L.	1/12/18 2/12/18		(No C Coy) Battalion remain in billets. General clean up and Batt. parade. Physical training and drill — at Company billets. "C" Coy (with 87th Bde.) remain at STAVELOT. (Armour 9. I.L.) Resuming parade.	
FRANCORCHAMPS (Sheet MARCHE 9) I.L.	3/12/18 4/12/18		The march to the frontier in continues, the Batt. (less C Coy) moving to FRANCORCHAMPS and 86th Bde. C Coy cross the Belgian-German frontier and march to ELSINGBURG LAGER (U.I.M.)	App. I. App. I.
WEISMES U.I.M.	5/12/18		Batt. (less C Coy) march to WEISMES, crossing the frontier at ROTHWASSER. "C" Coy march to LIVIERS at KONZEN (Sh. IL. Ref. IOG.)	App. 2.
MONTJOIE (Sh. IL. Ref. ILG.)	6/12/18		The march is continued to MONTJOIE via EISENBORN. C Coy proceed by march route with 87th Bde to SCHMIDT. (Sh.IL.Ref.8.I.)	App. 3.
NIDEGGAN (Sh.IL.Ref.8.J.)	7/12/18		Crossing by march route with 86th Bde., the Batt. reach NIDEGGAN. "C"Coy march to MÜLCK at LUXHEIM (Sh.IL.Ref.6L.)	App. 4.
ERP (Sh.IL.Ref.4N)	8/12/18		Batt. (less "C"Coy) marches to ERP via ZULPICH. "C" Coy move by march route to BRUGGEN. (Sh. IL. Ref. 4.N.)	App. 5.
SULZ (Sh.2L. Ref.2B)	9/12/18		The march is continued to SULZ (S.W. outskirts of COLOGNE). "C" Coy march incidentally to SULZ arriving in time to find all their places.	App. 6. App. 7.

Army Form C. 2118.

WAR DIARY
or
INTELLIGENCE SUMMARY.
(Erase heading not required.)

Instructions regarding War Diaries and Intelligence Summaries are contained in F. S. Regs., Part II. and the Staff Manual respectively. Title pages will be prepared in manuscript.

Place	Date	Hour	Summary of Events and Information	Remarks and references to Appendices
SULZ (Sh. 2L. Sq. 2B)	10/12/18		Bathing & cleaning parties. Issuing new clothing etc.	A
	12/12/18		Battalion marches to BERG GLADBACH crossing the R. RHINE by the HOHENZOLLERN BRIDGE. At the latter point the Batt reviewed fast the G.O.C. II Corps.	A
BERG GLADBACH (W.2L. Sq.1.E)	13/12/18			A
- do. -	14/12/18 to 20/12/18		Training at temporary billets - (P.T. and M.G. drill.)	A
STUMPF. (DOEBRINGHAUSEN) (J.2.K. Sq.10.F.)	21/12/18		In accordance with 29th Div. Oper: Order No 310, the Batt. proceeds by march route to area of DEBRINGHAUSEN and STUMPF. "B"& "C" Coys being billetted at the first-named village and "D" Coy and Batt HQ at the latter. "A" Coy billeted in ENNINGHAUSEN - (2 miles N.E.)	App. 8. A
- do. -	22/12/18 and 23/12/18		Parades at Coy billets which include P.T. and M.G. drill.	A
- do. -	24/12/18		A draft of 2 Officers and 60 O.R. arrived from base Depot.	A
- do. -	25/12/18		Xmas Day - No parades - Xmas dinners arranged by Companies. Followed by concerts at Coy billets.	A A
- do.	26/12/18		No parades.	A A

Army Form C. 2118.

WAR DIARY
or
INTELLIGENCE SUMMARY.
(Erase heading not required.)

Instructions regarding War Diaries and Intelligence Summaries are contained in F. S. Regs., Part II and the Staff Manual respectively. Title pages will be prepared in manuscript.

Place	Date	Hour	Summary of Events and Information	Remarks and references to Appendices
STUMPE & DEBRING HAUSEN	27/12/18		Lecture by Div. Educ. Officer to Officers + NCOs at Bn HQ. outlying Army Educ. Scheme	A
"	28/12/18		Passes granted to all ranks (up to 5% of strength) each day to visit Cologne 26th 27th & 28th Dec. A Coy bathing remainder P.T. & M.G. training. + 2 miners leave for demobilization	A
"	29/12/18		D coy bathing, no parades 7 miners leave for demobilization	A
"	30/12/18		B Coy bathing, P.T. & Education, + M.G. Trg. 5 miners leave for demobilization. Major Rendle (4 M.G. Bn) arrives for duty. also 8 drivers	A
"	31/12/18		C Coy bathing P.T. Education + M.G. Trg. 4 men (Watford Details) leave for demobilization	A

Sh. Tweeny Major.
LIEUT-COLONEL
COMDG. 29th BN. M.G. CORPS.

	Code	m.	Words.	Charge.	This message is on a/c of:	Recd. at	m.
Office of Origin and Service Instructions.			Sent		*Appended*	Date	
			At	m.	Service.	From	
			To			By	
			By		(Signature of " Franking Officer,")		

TO — MARCH TABLE for DEL

Sender's Number.	Day of Month.	In reply to Number.	AAA
*H40	30		

Unit	SP	Time	Route	Billets
1 RDF	Church	1100	DIEUPART	DESNE & BASSE DESNE
BHQ	at	1104	-SOUGNÉ	Chau Sq BANQUARD
1 L.F.	DIEUPART	1106	-REMOUCHAMPS	LA REID
13 RFA		1113	-HALTE	CREPPE
2 RF		1118	-X rds Wof "4 Fms on JOHOSTE"	BELLEVEAU Rd
		13 am		
510 RBt	form at	1210	BELLEVEAU	VERT BUISSON
89 FA	SOUGNÉ BRIDGE	1214	-Indapen	WINAMPLANCHE
24 MGC	remain at REMOUCHAMPS.			
No 2 Coy	independently MARTEAU 200 SE of 33KS on THEUX-SPA Rd			

Remarks
(1) 1 RDF to furnish adv Gd
(2) 2 Plns Pioneers to accompany Adv Gd
(3) CREPPE is only approachable via SPA
(4) ACKNOWLEDGE

From	88 Bde
Place	
Time	1130

Prefix .... Code .... m.	Words.	Charge.	This message is on a/c of:	Recd. at .... m.
Office of Origin and Service Instructions.	Sent			Date ....
	At .... m.		............Service.	From ....
	To		(Signature of "Franking Officer.")	By ....
	By			

TO MARCH TABLE for DEC 2

Sender's Number.	Day of Month.	In reply to Number.	AAA
* H 46	1		

Unit	SP	Time	Route
1 LF	Rd junc	1030	SPA
BHQ	junc's	1036	
1 RDF	of	1038	— FRANCO
13 RFA	33 K5	1044	RCHAMPS
2 RF	on THEUX	1049	
510 RE	— SPA	1106	
29 MGC	Rd	1110	
89 FA		1122	
No 2 Coy	Independently billet at FRANCORCHAMPS STN		

Remarks
1. 1 LF to furnish Adv Gd.
2. Billets are in FRANCORCHAMPS – STAVELOT AREA. Parties to meet SC at X rds FRANCORCHAMPS at 0930
3. ACKNOWLEDGE

From 86 Bde

Place

Time

The above may be forwarded as now corrected. (Z) G Heffernan

"A" Form
MESSAGES AND SIGNALS.

Army Form C. 2121
(In pads of 100.)

TO Mr G Bolton

Sender's Number.	Day of Month.	In reply to Number.	AAA
* H 50	1		

Tomorrow Dec 2nd Division will rest in present area aaa move ordered for tomorrow will take place on Dec 3rd aaa Date of March Table only altered aaa Acknowledge by bearer

From Place 8th Brigade

Jefferson
Major

"A" Form
MESSAGES AND SIGNALS.

Army Form C. 2121
(In pads of 100.)

No. of Message...............

Prefix............ Code............m | Words. | Charge. | This message is on a/c of: | Recd. at............m.
Office of Origin and Service Instructions | Sent | | | Date...............
....At................m. | | ....Service. | From...............
....To................ | | |
....By................ | | (Signature of "Franking Officer.") | By...............

TO   29 M G Bn

Sender's Number.   Day of Month.   In reply to Number.   AAA

* A 615   2/12

The Division will now remain in present area until Dec 4th aaa Move ordered for Dec. 3 will now take place Dec. 4th aaa acknowledge by bearer

From
Place   86 Bde.
Time

The above may be forwarded as now corrected.   (Z)

Censor.   Signature of Addressor or person authorized to telegraph in his name.
* This line should be erased if not required.

86th Inf. Bde. No. G4/58.

Copy No. 8

The following billeting areas are allotted to Units in the FRANCORCHAMPS - STAVELOT Area, on 4th December 1918:-

Brigade Headquarters	CHATEAU, MASTA, 300 yds N. of H 4n HAUSTA.
86th T.M. Battery	WAVREUMONT.
1st Lancs. Fusiliers) 2nd Royal Fusiliers)	MALMEDY.
1/R.Dub. Fusiliers	STER and CRONCHAMPS.
86th Bn. M.G.C.	FRANCORCHAMPS and ROTHWASSER.
510 Field Coy. R.E.	BURNENVILLE and MELZ.
15th Battery R.F.A.	CHENEUX and MISTA.
86th Field Ambulance	RIVAGE and BAS RIVAGE.
No. 2 Coy. A.S.C.	STATION, FRANCORCHAMPS.

Billeting Parties may now proceed independently without meeting Staff Captain first. Staff Captain will meet party of No. 2 Coy. at STATION, FRANCORCHAMPS at 09.45 and will be at MALMEDY CHURCH to allot areas to 1st Lancs.Fusiliers and 2nd Royal Fusiliers, at 10.30

Billeting Parties of 1st Lancs. Fusiliers and 2nd Royal Fusiliers must consist of 5 persons armed and mounted on horses or bicycles. The regulations regarding armed billeting parties laid down in this Office G.2/234 of the 1st instant will now come into force on 5th December.

C. Barrington Brown
Major,
A/Brigade Major,
86th Infantry Brigade.

2nd December 1918.

Copies to:-
1 - 3 Staff.
4 2/Royal Fusiliers.
5 1/Lancs. Fusiliers.
6 1/R.Dublin Fusiliers.
7 86th T.M.Battery.
8 86th Bn. M.G.Corps.
9 510th Field Coy. R.E.
10 86th Field Ambulance.
11 No. 2 Coy. 29th Div. Train.
12 15th Battery R.F.A.
13 Brigade Signal Officer.
14 B Coy. 1/? Mons Regt.
15 29th Division "G" (for Information).
16 Diary.
17 File.

I M. East ""
" West "
LT. BRAIN
John Laws

SECRET.   Appendix   Copy No. 12

86th INFANTRY BRIGADE ORDER No. 298

Ref: Sheets 1.K. and 1.L. 1/100,000.

3rd December 1918.

1. **INTENTION.**

    (a) On the 5th December the Brigade will march from the FRANCORCHAMPS – MALMEDY area to the WEISMES area.
    (b) Moves will be in accordance with Table attached.

2. **ADVANCE GUARD.**

    2 Coys   (a) Advance Guard as per margin will be in position at 10.00.
    2/R.Fus.   (b) Cyclists and Pioneers will report to O.C., Advance Guard at
    2 plats   starting point at 09.30.
    1/2 Horse   (c) Two platoons Pioneers with Advance Guard will halt in
    Regt.   BUTGENBACH.
    1 section (d) On arrival of Advance Guard at EISENBORN, the section of
    Cyclists.   Cyclists will establish communication with 87th Infantry
               Brigade at KAISER HERBERG and then return to Brigade
               Headquarters at NILBUM.

3. **OUTPOSTS.**

    (a) On completion of move the 2/Royal Fusiliers will picquet main roads leading East on front EISENBORN (incl) to KAISER HERBERG (excl) and will establish communication with 87th Infantry Brigade at KAISER HERBERG.
    (b) The 1/Lancs.Fusiliers will picquet the main roads East on front EISENBORN (excl) to BULLINGEN (excl) and establish communication with 1st Canadian Division at BULLINGEN.

4. **BILLETING PARTIES.**

    Parties will rendezvous at 08.00 on 5th December at MALMEDY STATION to meet Staff Captain.

5. **MOTOR CONVOY.**

    Motor Lorries will rendezvous at 11.15 at MALMEDY STATION.

6. **REPORTS.**

    Arrival in billets, locations, dispositions and marching-in states to be rendered by 18.00.

7. **GUARDS.**

    (a) O.C., 1/Lancs.Fusiliers will find any guards over wagons and convoys required by O.C., No.2 Coy. Train.
    (a) O.C. 29th M.G.Battalion will provide any guards required by O.C., 89th Field Ambulance.

8. ACKNOWLEDGE.

    Issued at,...............   Major,
                                                  A/Brigade Major,
                                                  86th Inf.Brigade.

Copies to:-
1 - 3 Staff.   13 1 Coy 1/2 Horse Regt.
4 - 5 2/Royal Fus.   14 15th Bty R.F.A.
6 1/Lancs.Fusiliers.   15 29th Division "G".
7 1/R.Dublin Fus.   16 M.T. Lorry Convoy.
8 29th M.G.Battery.   17 87th Inf.Brigade.
9 89th Field Ambulance.   18 Brigade Signal Officer.
10 29th Field Coy. R.E.   19 O.C. Cyclists.
11 No.2 Coy. Div.Train.   20 Diary.
12 29th D.A.C.Sectn.   21 File.

MARCH TABLE – issued in conjunction with Brigade Order 293

Serial No.	Unit.	S.P.	Time	Route	Billets
1	2/Roy.Fus. (less 2 Coys)	Point where railway cuts main road 1 mile East of MALMEDY STN.	10.15	BAUGNE – WEISMES, – ELSENBORN. BUTGENBACH.	
2	Bde H.Q. T.M.B.	do	10.19	do	NIDRUM
3	1/Lancs.Fus.	do	10.21	do	BUTGENBACH.
4	1/R.Dub.Fus.	do	10.26	do	WEYVERTZ
5	13/Bty R.F.A.	do	10.32	do	FAYMONVILLE.
6	510/Fld Coy RE.	do	10.37	do	WEISMES.
7	86th Bn. M.G.C.	do	10.41	do	WEISMES.
8	89th Field Ambce	do	11.10	do	WEISMES.
9	No.2 Coy. Train	do	11.13	do	BUTGENBACH.

MESSAGES AND SIGNALS.

Appendix 2

TO: A, B, D Coys, O.C.s and T.O. Rear

Sender's Number: BM 784 Day of Month: 4th

Orders for move tomorrow 5th inst are BnHQ will march E WEISMES via MALMEDY and BAUGNEZ are Distance about 5 miles. Will form up in order HQ A B and D Coys in Fighting formation followed by HQ Transport on road moving E through village. facing E with head of column at level crossing at Station are Ready to move at 08.40 hours are Blankets at QM 9 Shots 07.30 hours are Sick parade 06.45 hours are Dinners on arrival are Orders to billeting parties separately are ACK by bearer

From: 2nd Bn M.G. Corps
Place:
Time:

"A" Form
MESSAGES AND SIGNALS.

Army Form C. 2121
(in pads of 100.)

Prefix .... Code .... m.
Office of Origin and Service Instructions.

D.R.L.S.

Words. | Charge.
Sent
At .... m.
To
By

This message is on a/c of .
................................Service.
(Signature of "Franking Officer.")

Recd. at .... m.
Date
From
By

TO { A B C D } Coys — QM — TO — RSM

Sender's Number: BM 185
Day of Month: 4
In reply to Number: —
AAA

1) From tomorrow 5th inst Coys will take all precautionary measures as laid down aaa Coy limbers will all be parked together & a road guard from each Coy mounted immediately on arrival aaa In addition a guard will be mounted at Battn HQ by night being detailed from Coys in rotation aaa
2) From tomorrow the Battn will invariably march in fighting formation as laid down at BLARINGHEM (i.e. Subsections behind coy limbers) aaa
3) Coys are reminded of instructions re carrying of arms etc aaa

From: 29th Bn M.G. Corps
Place:
Time:

The above may be forwarded as now corrected. (Z)
....
Censor. | Signature of Addressor or person authorised to telegraph in his name.
* This line should be erased if not required.
(1539). Wt. W2253/P511. 200,000 Pads. 2/18. H.C.&L., Ltd.

Army Form C. 2121
(in pads of 100.)

...AND SIGNALS.

Prefix ...... Code ...... m.	Words.	Charge.	This message is on a/c of.	Recd. at ...... m.
Office of Origin and Service Instructions.	Sent		..................Service.	Date ......
DR66	At.........m.			From ......
Rf Sheet 1M	To			
	By		(Signature of "Franking Officer.")	By

TO { A, B, D } Cups Qm and TO R/m

| Sender's Number. | Day of Month. | In reply to Number. | AAA |
| BK 786 | 4th | — | |

Orders for Billeting parties for Dec 5th are OC A Coy will detail one Section to proceed complete with arms and transport with Billeting parties AAA This section will be at level crossing ready to move at 06.30 hours AAA Usual parties will report to 2/Lt GADSBY at same time and place AAA Parties will proceed under Senior Officer reporting Staff Captn. MALMEDY STN. at 08.00 hours AAA 2/Lt GADSBY will clear areas in WEISMES as usual AAA ACKNOWLEDGE by bearer

From Place: 29th Bn. M.G. Corps

Time

The above may be forwarded as now corrected. (Z) _____ Capt.

Censor.   Signature of Addressor or person authorised to telegraph in his name.

* This line should be erased if not required.

29th Div. No. G.G.S. 45/205.

88th Inf.Bde.Group.
86th Inf.Bde.Group.
87th Inf.Bde.Group.
"Q"

6th December 1918.

----

1.   On the 9th instant the M.G. and Pioneer Coys. with the leading Bdes. will rejoin their Battns. The former in 86th Inf.Bde. the latter in 87th Inf.Bde. area – under arrangements to be made between B.Gs.

2.   B.G.C. 88th Inf.Bde. will please arrange to billet his M.G. and Pioneer Coys. forward on the night 9th/10th. These units will march direct to their units on the 10th via LIBLAR. B.Gs.C. 86th and 87th Inf.Bdes. will detail guides to be at cross roads 1 mile E.N.E. of E.in NFFFRFN at 1200.

Lieut-Colonel, G.S.
29th Division.

3.

Copies to :- 29th Battn.M.G.Corps.
             1/2 Monmouth Regt. (P).

"A" Form
MESSAGES AND SIGNALS.

Army Form C. 2121 (in pads of 100.)

Prefix .... Code .... m. | Words. | Charge. | This message is on a/c of: | Recd. at .... m.
Office of Origin and Service Instructions. | Sent | | .... Service. | Date ....
.... | At .... m. | | | From ....
.... | To .... | | (Signature of "Franking Officer.") | By ....
.... | By .... | | |

TO: MARCH TABLE for DEC 6

Sender's Number	Day of Month	In reply to Number	AAA
* H51	4		

Unit	SP	Time	Route	Billets
2RF	ELSEN	0945	ELSEN	EILHERSEHEID
BHQ	ELSEN	1000	BORN	KONZEN
1RDF	BORN	1002	KALTER	SIMMERATH
1LF	X rds	1008	HERBERG	MUTZENICH
13RFA		1014	MOUNTJOIE	IMGENBROICHE
29MGC		1018	IMGEN	MOUNTJOIE
510 RE		1031	BROICHE	MOUNTJOIE
89 FA		1035		MOUNTJOIE
No 2 Coy		1038		KONZEN / MOUNTJOIE

REMARKS

(1) Adv Gd 2 Coys 2RF. No pioneers required
(2) All 4 Battns to picket main roads E in Billeting Area
(3) Rendezvous for Billeting parties on Dec 6 will be ELSENBORN X rds at 0800
(4) 1 RDF from SIMMERATH to establish Comm'd with 87 Bde or DHQ at STECKENBORN
(5) ACKNOWLEDGE

G Heffernan Maj
2/131788 Bde

Prefix .... Code ....m.	Words.	Charge.	This message is on a/c of.	Recd. at ....m.
Office of Origin and Service Instructions.	Sent			
DRLS	At........m.		........Service.	Date ....
Ref. 1M	To			From ....
...... 1L	By		(Signature of "Franking Officer.")	By ....

TO { A / B / C / D } Corps QM and TO RSM

Sender's Number.	Day of Month.	In reply to Number.	AAA
* BK 788	5th		

Orders for move for 6th December
are being marched to
MONTJOIE via BUTGENBACH —
ELSENBORN — KALTER HERBERG
Distance about 16 miles
Troops same order as today on
road moving N. through villages
facing N. with head of column
at road junction 500x NW of W in
WEISMES are Ready to move
at 07.15 hours Blankets
QM Stores 06.15 hours Sick
Parades 06.00 hours ACKNOWLEDGE

From: 29th Bn M.G. Corps
Place:
Time:

The above may be forwarded as now corrected. (Z)

Censor. Signature of Addressee or person authorised to telegraph in his name.
* This line should be erased if not required.
(1539). Wt. W2253/P511. 200,000 Pads. 2/18. H.C.&L., Ltd.

MESSAGES AND SIGNALS.

Prefix	Code	m.	Words.	Charge.	This message is on a/c of.	Recd. at .... m.
Office of Origin and Service Instructions.			Sent		.........................Service.	Date ....
DRLS			At.............m.			From ....
Ref Sheets 1L			To			
1M.			By		(Signature of "Franking Officer.")	By ....

TO	A/C B/Coy D/	QM & TO	RSM	

Sender's Number.	Day of Month.	In reply to Number.	
*MK 789	5		AAA

Orders for billetting parties for 6th Bn. AAA Owing to long distance to Brigade rendez-vous no M.G. section will proceed with billetting party AAA All cyclists in Batt. with exception of one HQ runner will proceed in addition to usual parties AAA Senior officer will form into one body & take charge reporting to Staff Capt. at X RDS ELSENBORN at 08.00 hours AAA All ranks will be fully armed AAA Above parties rendezvous at CHURCH WEISMES at 06.30 hours AAA ACKNOWLEDGE

From	29th Bn. M.G. Corps
Place	
Time	

The above may be forwarded as now corrected. (Z)
Censor. Signature of Addressor or person authorised to telegraph in his name.
* This line should be erased if not required.

TO: **MARCH TABLE for Dec 7**

Sender's Number.	Day of Month.	In reply to Number.	AAA
H 60	5		

Unit	SP	Time	Route
1 RDF	4 Rd Junc	0945	SIMMERATH
BHQ	Just N of	1000	- STRAUCH
2 RF	Km	1003	- SCHMIDT
1 LF	-	1009	- NIDEGGAN
13 RFA	KESTERNICH	1015	
29 MGC		1019	
516 RE		1032	
89 FA		1036	
No 2 Coy		1040	

Remarks

1. Adv Gd. 2 Coys 1 RDF
2. Rendezvous for billeting parties Rd Junc just N of Rm SIMMERATH at 0800 aaa Btd representatives must be punctual even if main parties are delayed
3. Exact billets of units not yet known
4. Rd out of MOUNTJOIE is very stiff
5. Lorries to be at SIMMERATH at 1130

G. Heffernan

"A" Form
MESSAGES AND SIGNALS.

Army Form C. 2121
(In pads of 100)

TO	A) B) Coys QM and TO RSM D)

Sender's Number: BK 798
Day of Month: 6
AAA

Orders for move for 7th December are Battn marches to NIDEGGAN via IMGENBROICH - SIMMERATH - STRAUCH - SCHMIDT aaa Distance about 17 miles aaa Form up in same order as today on road running N from R in BURGAU to W in WEISENTHAL with head of column at latter point facing N aaa Ready to move at 07.45 hours aaa Blankets QM Stores 06.45 hours aaa Sick parade 06.00 hours aaa Billeting parties report 2/Lt GADSBY and All Bn Cyclists as today aaa CHURCH at 06.30 hours aaa Tea and haversack rations on march dinners on arrival aaa ACKNOWLEDGE

From / Place: 9th Bn HQ Coys

"A" Form
MESSAGES AND SIGNALS.

Army Form C. 2121
(In pads of 100.)

TO: 29 M.G Bn.

Sender's Number: 462
Day of Month: 6

Billets tomorrow allotted as follows:-

1 RDF	EMBKEN
2 RF	BOICH
1 LF	THUM
MG Bn }	NIDEGGEN
89 FA }	"
B'HQ }	
T.M.B }	WOLLERSHEIM
No 2 Coy }	
510 (Ay RE)	BERG
RFA	WOLLERSHEIM

From
Place: 86 Infy Bde
Time:

Major

MESSAGES AND SIGNALS

118 Bns.

TO: MARCH TABLE for Dec 8

Sender's Number: 167 Day of Month: 6

Unit	SP	Time	Route	Billets
1LF	Rd	0945	FROITZHEIM)	LECHENICH
BHQ	June	1000	VETTWEISS)	
1RDF	100×S	1002	- ERP)	
2RF	offst	1008		AHREM
13RFA	6 in	1014		HERRIG
510BE	Froitz	1019		ERP
No 2 Coy	heim	1023		LECHENICH
29MGC		1027		ERP
84FA		1040		ERP

Remarks
1) Adv Gd 2 Coys 1LF
2) 1RDF to picket roads E of LECHENICH
3) Billeting representatives to meet SC at FROITZHEIM church 0830
4) Lorries to rendezvous FROITZHEIM 11.30
5) Halt from 1215 to 1300

From: 86 Bde

G Heffernan
Major

"A" Form
MESSAGES AND SIGNALS.

Prefix........ Code. *........m	Words.	Charge.	This message is on a/c of:	Recd. at............m.
Office of Origin and Service Instructions	Sent			Date..................
...DRLS............	At............m.		............Service.	From..................
Ref. Sheet 12	To............			
............................By		(Signature of "Franking Officer.")	By..................

TO	A	Coy	Qm and T.O. RSM	
	B			
	D			

Sender's Number: 604
Day of Month: 7
In reply to Number:
AAA

Orders for move. One December 8th has Battn marches to ERP via THUM – KROTZHEIM – VETTWEISS. Distance about 14 miles. Form up in order as today on NIDEGGEN – THUM road (moving under own) with head of column at road junction at I in NIDEGGEN and Ready to move at 08.30 hours. Blankets RM times 07.30 hours. Sick parades 06.45 hours. Billeting parties and cyclists report to GADSBY in charge at 07.00 hours. ... as today ... Dinners on arrival. ACKNOWLEDGE

From: 2nd Bn ... Coys
Place:
Time:

The above may be forwarded as now corrected. (Z)
Censor. Signature of Addressor or person authorised to telegraph in his name.
* This line should be erased if not required.

"A" Form
MESSAGES AND SIGNALS.
Army Form C. 2121
(In pads of 100)

TO	A B C D	Coy	Coy and TO	RSM

Sender's Number: BK 805
Day of Month: 8
In reply to Number: -
AAA

Ref my BK 804 one Battn
will move from u/s on BORG wood
to area E will head of road
junction just clear of NIDEGGEN
move at 08.30 hours Ack
Recd 175012 1159 M
impossible Ack

From 29 Bn HQ Coy

Form
MESSAGES AND SIGNALS.
Army Form C. 2121 (in pads of 100.)

TO MARCH TABLE for 8th DECEMBER 1918.

Sender's Number.	Day of Month.	In reply to Number.	
* H.71	7		AAA

Unit	S.P.	Time	Route	Billets.
1/S.D.F.	Rd Junc.	09.00	LIBLAR —)	SULZ and
B.H.Q.	A in S.	09.05	EPPERUN —)	S.W. Out-
1/L.F.	of First	09.08	SULZ)	skirts of
2/S.F.	C in	09.16	)	KOLN.
137/R.F.A.	LECHENICH.	09.25	)	
510/F.E.		09.28	)	
No. 3 Train		09.32	)	
89/F.A.		09.36	)	
29/M.G.C.		09.40	)	

REMARKS. one
1. Adv. Guard ∧ Coys 1/R.D.F.
2. Billeting representatives to meet G.C. at LECHENICH CHURCH at 08.00.
3. Orders regarding pickets etc will be issued separately.
4. Lorries to rendezvous LECHENICH at 11.00.
5. No halt for dinner.
6. D.H.Q. will be at EPPERUN.
7. Rest on 10th, 11th and 12th.

Place: 86th Brigade.

Major

MESSAGES AND SIGNALS.

TO: A, B, C [Bde] Cmrs and T.O. R.S.M.

Sender's Number: BM 607 Day of Month: 8 2 AAA

Orders for move for Dec 9th are AAA B-lin marches to SULZ (Sw. outskirts of KÖLN) via LECHENICH — main road AAA Distance about 16½ miles AAA Form up in usual order on road running NE through village with head of column at road junction 500x N of E in ERP AAA Ready to move at 08.25 hours AAA Blankets Own stores 07.30 hours AAA Sick parade 06.45 hours AAA Billeting parties and cyclists under 2/Lt GODBY at CHURCH at 07.00 hours AAA Tea on march dinners on arrival AAA Acknowledge

From: 2yth Bde Arty. Corps

MESSAGES AND SIGNALS.

TO: 29 Batt. MGC

Sender's Number: H77
Day of Month: 8

C Coy now attached to 87 Brigade will join you in your billeting area at SULZ tomorrow Dec 9

From: 86 Bde

G. Heffernan
Major

MESSAGES AND SIGNALS

TO: 29 B'n MGC

Sender's Number: H 74
Day of Month: 8

AAA

Tomorrow Dec 9 The Coy of your B'n attached to 87 Brigade will rejoin you in the Suez area aaa Details will be notified you as soon as arranged

From: 86 Bde

G Heffernan
Major

Appendix 8

Copy No. 14

29th DIVISION OPERATION ORDER No. 310.

Ref. Map 2Z and 2K.
and Map "A".

19th December 1918.

1. The 29th Div. area and the allotment of sub-areas within, is as shown on attached Map "A". (not attached)

2. The Division will be concentrated in the above area by 1200 on 21st December in accordance with attached march table.
 Orders for taking and handing over the forward part of WIPPERFELD, WERMELS KERCHEM, REMSCHEID and CRONENBERG sub-areas will be issued later. (Shewn on map "A" by dotted lines).

3. (a) Subject to para.2 Sub-Area Commandants will take over where not already done, the administration of their sub-areas from 1200 21st instant, but will allow troops of other Brigades located in these areas to remain for the present.

 (b) On 21st instant, 86th Inf.Brigade will hand over posts in the vicinity of LINDE to 1st Canadian Division by 1200. (Further instructions will be issued from this Office).

4. Details of billets in BERG GLADBACH will be arranged by 29th Division "Q" Staff.

5. D.H.Q. will close at HENSBERG and open at SAND Chateau at 1200 on 21st instant.

6. ACKNOWLEDGE.

Lieut-Colonel, G.S.
29th Division.

S.

Issued at 2030

Distribution.

	Copy No.		Copy No.
G.O.C.	1	D.A.P.M.	21
G.S.	2-3	D.A.D.O.S.	22
"Q".	4-5	Camp Commandant.	23
C.R.A.	6-7	29th Div.M.T.Coy.	24
C.R.E.	8	226th Div.Emplyt.Coy.	25
Signals.	9	Canteen Officer.	26
86th Inf.Bde.	10-11	Middlesex Transport.	27
87th Inf.Bde.	12-13	II Corps.	28-29
88th Inf.Bde.	14-15	1st Canadian Division.	30
1/2 Mcr.Regt. (P).	16	1st Cavalry Division.	31
29th Bn.M.G.Corps.	17	New Zealand Division.	32
Div.Train.	18	9th Division.	33
A.D.M.S.	19	War Diary.	34-35
D.A.D.V.S.	20		

P.T.O.

M A R C H   T A B L E.   (To accompany 29th Div. Order No. 310).

Serial No.	Date.	Unit.	From area.	To area.	Route.	Remarks.
1.	Dec. 21st	29th Bn.M.G.Corps.	BERG GLADBACH	VITZHELDEN	HEBBORN-ODENTHAL-HOLZ-BLECHER-KALTER-HERBERG.	Clear GLADBACH by 09.45. See No.5.
2.	-do-	29th D.A. H.Q. Group. 29th D.A.C. 58th A.F.A.Bde.	DELLBRUCK	BERG GLADBACH	Any.	(a) Move to be completed and roads clear by 1100. (b) Not to reach cross rds. ½ mile S. of E. of H in BERG GLADBACH before 0945.
3.	-do-	17th Bde.R.F.A.	BENSBERG East.	BERG GLADBACH	HERKENRATH-SAND.	(a) Not to reach GLADBACH before 0945. (b) Move to be completed and rds.clear by 1100. (c) Move under orders of C.R.A.
4.	-do-	80th Inf.Bde. Group (less 1 Bn.)	BENSBERG	BERG GLADBACH	BENSBERG-BERG GLADBACH.	(a) To clear BENSBERG by 1045. (b) Not to reach GLADBACH before 1100. (c) Move to be completed by 1145. (d) Bde.H.Q. move independently to ODENTHAL Chateau.

P. T. O.

Serial No.	Date	Unit	From area	To area	Route	Remarks
5.	Dec. 21st	1/2nd Mcn.R.(P)	SIEBEN MORGEN	BURSCHEID	BENSBERG – GLADBACH thence as for Serial No.1.	(a) Not to reach BENS- BERG before 1100 and clear it by 1120. (b) Not to reach GLAD- BACH before 1200. (c) Road from Cross- roads ¾ mile N.W. of 1st B in BENSBERG to GRONAU, not available.
6.	-do-	D.H.Q.	BENSBERG	SAND	BENSBERG to Cross roads ¾ mile N.W. of first B in BENSBERG.	(a) Not to enter road before 1130. (b) To clear BENSBERG by 1200.

NOTE - Transport of Serials 1 and 5 to move from GLADBACH via PAFFRATH and SCHLEBUSCH.

S E C R E T.   COPY NO. 10

29th BN. M.G. CORPS.
Operation Order No. 47

Ref: Sheets 2.L. and 2.K., 1/100,000.

1. The Battn. will march complete tomorrow 21st December to DABRINGHAUSEN (E. of BURSCHEID) via ODENTHAL and ALTENBERG. Distance about 10 miles.

2. The Battn. will form up in order H.Q., "A", "B", "C" and "D" Coys. and H.Q. Transport on HERRENSTUNDEN - BERG GLADBACH Road facing W. with head of column at corner of BENSBERG Road. Column to be ready to move at 09.30 hours.

3. Battn. will march in normal M.G.Battn. formation (sub-sections behind limbers) with intervals of 30 yards between Coys. and 30 yards between Rear Coy. and H.Q. Transport.

4. Billetting parties (armed) will meet 2/Lieut. GADSBY in the Square, BERG GLADBACH, at 07.30 hours.

5. Tea and haversack rations on the march. Dinners on arrival.

6. Sick parades will be at 07.30 hours.

7. All billets and horse lines will be left thoroughly clean. Os.C. Coys. will pay special attention to this.

8. Orders regarding blankets will be issued later. Coys. will be prepared to carry them on limbers.

9. ACKNOWLEDGE.

20th December 1918.

Major,
Comdg 29th Bn. M.G.Corps.

Copies to:
1. "A" Coy.
2. "B" "
3. "C" "
4. "D" "
5. Q.M. & Sigs.Officer.
6. Battn.T.O.
7. 29th Div.G.(for information)
8.)
9.) File.
10.)
11.) War Diary.

2/14 A. F. Gadsby

"C" FORM.
MESSAGES AND SIGNALS.

Army Form C. 2123.
(In books of 100.)
No. of Message..........

Prefix....... Code....... Words.......	Sent, or sent out.	Office Stamp.
Received from...... By......	At.............m.	MB0
Service Instructions	To............. By......	20.12.18

Handed in at ...YB1... Office ...1745... m. Received ...1755... m.

TO 29th Bn M/Corps

*Sender's Number.	Day of Month.	In reply to Number.	AAA
F374	20th		
Ref	Divn	order	310
dated	19th	29th	Bn
M/	Corps	will	move
to	DABRINGHAUSEN	and	
not	as	stated	

FROM PLACE & TIME 29th Div G
1700

RHINE ARMY
SOUTHERN DIVISION
LATE 29TH DIVISION

BTN
29TH MACHINE GUN COY.
JAN-OCT 1919

Box 2069 & 2084

Vol. 12

WAR DIARY.

29TH BATTALION.
Machine Gun Corps.
1st – 31st January 1919.

WAR DIARY
INTELLIGENCE SUMMARY

Army Form C. 2118.

(Erase heading not required.)

Place	Date	Hour	Summary of Events and Information	Remarks and references to Appendices
DABRINGHAUSEN	1/1/19		All companies M.G. & Educational Trg. B. Coy came but entries one hour P.T.	
STUNPF	2/1/19		All companies inspected by C.O. at 09.00 hrs. then proceed for route march	
Start 3.9.			STUMPF, GRUNEWALD, DHONENBURG, SCHIRPENDHUVN, ENGERFELD, DADINGHAUSEN.	
COLN			3 Officers & 2 "Guarantee Letter" men left for demobilization	
"	3/1/19		A,B,C, & D Coy M.G. & Educational Trg. P.T. for A.C. Companies	
"	4/1/19		A Coy move from EMMINGHAUSEN to DABRINGHAUSEN & take over billets which	
			were occupied by a detachment of two Labour Coy.	Appendix I
"	5/1/19		Reinforcement of 45 OR's from Bn.	
			Parade Service for all nonconformists in Church at DABING-HAUSEN.	
"	6/1/19		All companies M.G. & Educational Trg. C. & D. Coys P.T. divine service for Danks.	
"	7/1/19		Do. A & B Coys P.T.	
"	8/1/19		All companies M.G. & Educational Trg. A & B Coys P.T.	
"	9/1/19		Do. C. & D. Coys P.T.	
"	10/1/19		Do. C. Coy Boxing	
"	11/1/19		Practice for Ceremonial Parade. H.Q. backing. 14 OR's & 2 Officers leave for demobilization	

Army Form C. 2118.

WAR DIARY
INTELLIGENCE SUMMARY.
(Erase heading not required.)

Instructions regarding War Diaries and Intelligence Summaries are contained in F. S. Regs., Part II. and the Staff Manual respectively. Title pages will be prepared in manuscript.

Place	Date	Hour	Summary of Events and Information	Remarks and references to Appendices
DABRINGHAUSEN SHEET 59	12/1/19		Church Parade at Church Dabringhausen for all Coy.	
	13/1/19		All Coy under Coy arrangements militty PT. M.O. Examination & Recreation 19 men leave for demobilization.	A
COLN				A
	14/1/19		On parade for Inspection of rifles & clothes by Div. Cmdr at 10.15. Lunch Inspection of billets by Div. Cmdr. 13 men leave for demobilization. 60 or more as reinforcements.	A
	15/1/19		All Coy under Coy arrangements. P.T. M.S. Education & Recreation.	A
	16/1/19		Do. Officers & Transport & horses under R.S.M. 15 m.r Bain	A
	17/1/19		R.H.A. for moving Inspection. lines. Coy arrangements P.T. M.S. Education & Recreation. Officers Riding for 1 hour.	A
	18/1/19		Do	A
	19/1/19		Church Parade for Left. at Dabringhausen. 1 Officer + 28 or more for demobilization	A
	20/1/19		Coy arrangement. P.T. M.S. Education & Recreation. Officers Riding. 80 or more for reinforcement. 6 or more for demobilization.	A
	21/1/19		All Coy under Coy arrangements militty PT. M.S. Education & Recreation. Officers Riding. 1 Officer + 36 o.r. leave for demobilization.	A
	22/1/19		All Coys under Coy arrangements including P.T. M.S. Education & Recreation. 4 Officers + 47 o.r. leave for demobilization.	A

WAR DIARY or INTELLIGENCE SUMMARY

Army Form C. 2118.

Place	Date	Hour	Summary of Events and Information	Remarks and references to Appendices
DABRINGHAUSEN & STUMPF. SHEET S.9	23/1/19		P.T., M.G., Lewis Gun and Bayonet training under Coy. arrangements	App.
	24/1/19		3 O.R.s from Battalion sent for Brit Army exams carried out by all Coys	
CÖLN	25/1/19		General Malone gave General Lecture and training	App.
			3 O.R.s leave for Dunkirk	
do	26/1/19		L.F.T. and R.C. Church Parades. Church entertainment in the evening at STUMPF. Lectures	App.
do	27/1/19		Till 8 am wet at Rainy - (P.T. M.G. - Lewis gun Bayonet) - Other Mouldish	App.
do	28.1.19 to 31.1.19		Parades as above carried out under company arrangements	App.

Appendix I

<u>SECRET.</u>

O.C., "A" Coy. 29th Bn. M.G. Corps.
No.5 Labour Coy.
Q.M., 29th Bn. M.G. Corps) for information.

----

1.   "A" Coy., 29th Bn. M.G. Corps and No.5 Labour Coy. will exchange billeting areas tomorrow 4th inst.

2.   Each Company will clear its area by 10.00 hours.

3.   O.C., "A" Coy., 29th Bn. M.G. Corps will arrange all details regarding billeting, etc., and report completion of move by phone.

4.   "A" Coy., 29th Bn. M.G. Corps to ACKNOWLEDGE.

RD/188.

3rd January 1919.   Major,
                            Comdg 29th Bn. M.G. Corps.

"C" FORM.
MESSAGES AND SIGNALS.

Army Form C. 2123.
(In books of 100.)
No. of Message..........

Prefix **SP** Code **9000** Words **58**

Sent, or sent out.
At............m.
To............m.
By

Office Stamp.
MBS
2/1/18

Received from............ By............
Service Instructions **Priority**

Handed in at **YB1** Office **9000** m. Received **2010** m.

TO **29 By mgc**

Sender's Number.	Day of Month.	In reply to Number.	AAA
F.444	2nd	Jan.	the
by	"		at
machine	gun	company	at
EMERSHAUSEN		will	move
to	DABRINGSHAUSEN		
and	change	over	with
the	Infantry	company	at
latter	place	aaa	O.C
mg	Bn	will	arrange
for	relief	Infantry	company
at	former	place	aaa
Acknowledge		aaa	
addressed		29 mg Bn	
repeated	14th	Labour	company
" Q "		and 88th Inf Bde	

FROM
PLACE & TIME **29 Div 1930**

* This line, except A A A, should be erased, if not required.

M 13

WAR DIARY.

29TH BATTN.

MACHINE GUN CORPS.

1ST TO 28TH FEBRUARY, 1919.

DUPLICATE

Army Form C. 2118.

WAR DIARY
or
INTELLIGENCE SUMMARY.
(Erase heading not required.)

Instructions regarding War Diaries and Intelligence Summaries are contained in F. S. Regs., Part II. and the Staff Manual respectively. Title pages will be prepared in manuscript.

Place	Date	Hour	Summary of Events and Information	Remarks and references to Appendices
STOMPF & DABRINGHAUSEN SHEET 2X F/10	1-2-19		Training (P.T., Y.S. & Recreational Training) at Coy drills.	
-do-	2-2-19		No parades - sports.	
-do-	3-2-19		Usual Training under Coy arrangements including P.T. Y.S. Recreational & Educational Training	
-do-	8-2-19		C.E. Church parade for all boys of Recreation Room - DABRINGHAUSEN spots.	
-do-	9-2-19		in afternoon 2 O.R.s from Battalion for Base. 1 officer to UK for demobilisation.	
-do-	10-2-19		Usual training under Coy arrangements including P.T. Y.S. Recreational & Educational Training.	
-do-	11-2-19		Usual training under Coy arrangements including P.T. Y.S. Recreational & Educational Training.	
-do-	12-2-19		Route March. DABRINGHAUSEN, STUMPF, GRUNEWALD, KAFRINGHAUSEN, HASERFELD, DABRINGHAUSEN about 10 kilos.	
-do-	13-2-19		Usual training under Coy arrangements. 1 officer to UK for disposal.	
-do-	14-2-19		Cross Country Run, about 2½ miles starting from KRANZHAUSEN. Usual educational training	
-do-	15-2-19		Usual training under Coy arrangements including P.T. Y.S. Recreational Educational Training	
-do-	16-2-19		C.E. Church parade for all Coys at STUMPF. Non-conformist Church parade at DABRINGHAUSEN	
-do-	17-2-19		Usual training under Coy arrangements including P.T. Y.S. Recreational Educational training	
			One Officer struck off strength whilst on leave & UK pending clerical.	
-do-	18/2/19		Usual P.T. Y.S. Recreational & Educational Training under Coy arrangements	

WAR DIARY
or
INTELLIGENCE SUMMARY.

(Erase heading not required.)

Army Form C. 2118.

Place	Date	Hour	Summary of Events and Information	Remarks and references to Appendices
STUMPF ?				
INSINGHAUS-	19.2.19		Manual P.T., M.G., Recreational & Educational training under Coy. arrangements.	
EN.				
Stpt. J.K.	20.2.19		Manual P.T, M.G. Recreational & Educational training under Coy. arrangements.	
Germany.				
F.10.	21.2.19		Cross country run, about 3 miles, starting from ARNZHAUSEN at 12.00 hrs. Manual	
"			Educational training.	
"	22.2.19		Manual P.T., M.G. Recreational & Educational training under Coy. arrangements.	
"	23-28.2.19	09.30	C.E. Church parade at INSINGHAUSEN for all Coys.	
"			Manual P.T., M.G. (laying, sightsetting, J.A. and mechanism) Recreational & Educational training	
"	24.2.19		under Coy. arrangements.	
"	25.2.19		Manual P.T., M.G., recreational & educational training under Coy. arrangements.	
"	26.2.19.		Manual P.T., M.G., recreational & educational training under Coy. arrangements.	
"	28.2.19		Manual P.T., M.G., Recreational & Educational training under Coy. arrangements.	

LIEUT.-COLONEL,
COMDG. 29th BN. M.G. CORPS.

29th Bn M.G. Corps.

Army Form C. 2118.

WAR DIARY
or
INTELLIGENCE SUMMARY.
(Erase heading not required.)

Place	Date	Summary of Events and Information	Remarks and references to Appendices
STUMPF. DABRINGHAUSEN. GRUNEWALD.	1919 MAY 1.	Training under Company arrangements, including gun drill, educational & recreational training	
	2nd	" " " " "	
	3rd	" " " " "	
	4th	C & D Coys. Church Parade at 10.30 at Recreation Room. 'A' & 'B' Coys. in Church at DABRINGHAUSEN at 12.10. Voluntary Holy Communion & Evening Services were held.	
	5th	Training under Company arrangements, including Range practices, educational & Recreational Training. One man rejd. from Hospital.	
	6th	Training as for 5th inst. That to DABRINGHAUSEN by H.R.H. Duke of CONNAUGHT at 16.00 hrs. One man joined 182 from 56th Bn. M.G.C.	
	7th	Training as for 6th inst. Twenty O.R. sent to U.K. for dispersal (including 2 time serving soldiers) Visit to DABRINGHAUSEN by H.R.H. Duke of CONNAUGHT at 16.00 hrs.	
	8th	Training as per 7th inst. Cross-country race between Companies.	
	9th	" " " " "	
	10th	" " " " "	
	11th	C & D Coys. Church Parade at 10.30 in Recreation Room. 'A' & 'B' Coys in Church at DABRINGHAUSEN at 12.10. Voluntary Holy Communion & Evening Services were held.	

WAR DIARY
or
INTELLIGENCE SUMMARY.
(Erase heading not required.)

Army Form C. 2118.

Sheet 2.

Place	Date	Hour	Summary of Events and Information	Remarks and references to Appendices
	12th		Training as per 10th inst.	4/MB
	13th		" " " " " "	4/MB
	14th		Three Officers struck off strength (To U.K. for dispersal)	4/MB
	15th		" " " " " "	4/MB
	16		" " " " " "	4/MB
	17		" " " " " " Batn Concert Party gave performance at 18.00 hrs at DABRINGHAUSEN. One man joined Batn from Base.	4/MB
	18		C & D Coys Church Parade at Recreation Room (10.30 hrs). A & B at Church in DABRINGHAUSEN (12.10 hrs). Voluntary Holy Communion Evening Service were held.	4/MB
	19		Training as per 17th inst.	4/MB
	20		" " " " " "	4/MB
	21st		" " " " " " 50 O.R. to U.K. for dispersal struck off strength.	4/MB
	22nd		" " " " " " $44	4/MB
	23rd		Training hours reduced to four per day as from this date. 100 O.R + 5 Officers posted to Bn from 34th 18th M.G.B. Battn concert at DABRINGHAUSEN	4/MB
	24		" as per 23rd inst: One atd. N.C.O. (R.A.V.C.) to U.K. for dispersal @ 18.00 hrs	4/MB

Army Form C. 2118.

WAR DIARY
or
INTELLIGENCE SUMMARY. Sheet 3
(Erase heading not required.)

Place	Date	Hour	Summary of Events and Information	Remarks and references to Appendices
	25th		C & D Coys Church parade at Recreation Room at 1030 hrs. A & B Coys in Church at DABRINGHAUSEN at 12.10. (Voluntary Holy Communion & Evening Services were held.) 2 O.R. Joined from Base.	
	26th		Training as per 24th inst. 3 O.R. transferred to U.K. as having re-enlisted, & for re-enlistment leave. Batt. football team matched against 24th Hampshire Regt. at WERMELSKIRCHEN resulting in a victory for the latter team. 162 O.R. & 5 Officers posted from 34 Bn. M.G. Corps.	
	27th		Training as per 26th.	
	28th		" " " " One man struck off strength (died nothing on)	
	29th		Leave to U.K. 26/2/19). One Officer joined from 34th Bn. M.G.C.	
	30th		Training as per 28th	
	31st		" " " Batt. Concert Party performance at DABRINGHAUSEN.	

[signature]
Capt. & Adjt.
29th Bn. M.G. Corps.

Army Form C. 2118.

WAR DIARY
or
INTELLIGENCE SUMMARY.
(Erase heading not required.)

29/M.G.

Place	Date	Hour	Summary of Events and Information	Remarks and references to Appendices
STUMPF & DABRINGHAUSEN.	1st		Church Parades – C and D Companies, in Recreation Room STUMPF and A and B Companies, in Lutheran Church DABRINGHAUSEN. Vol. Holy Communion and Evening Services were held.	
	2nd	09.15 – 13.00 Hours.	1 attached O.R. (R.A.O.C.) sent to U.K. for dispersal. Part 1 on Short Range. Educational and Recreational Training.	
	3rd	do.	Training as per 2nd inst. 1 O.R. Posted from 37th Battalion M.G.Corps. 2 O.R. struck off strength (sick in U.K.)	
	4th	do.	Parades as per 2nd inst. 1 D.R. to Educational Course in U.K. and struck off strength. Cricket Match.	
	5th	09.15 – 13.00 hours.	Recreational Educational and Machine Gun Training.	
	6th	do.	Parades as per 5th inst. for men not proceeding to Southern Divisional Races, held in Cologne. 2 places in Mule Race. 1 Officer and 1 O.R. joined from 37th Battalion M.G.Corps.	
	7th		As per 6th. Continuation of Divisional Race meeting.	
	8th		Church Parades – As per 1st inst. 4 O.R. posted from Base. 2 O.R. struck off strength (to U.K. re-enl. and 1 O.R. to R.P.O. 1 O.R. re-posted to 51st Bn.M.G.Corps. 1 Officer to U.K. for repatriation.	
	9th		Usual Training including short Range work. 1 Officer to U.K. for repatriation.	
	10th		Training as per previous day. Cricket Committee formed.	
	11th		Usual Training including Machine Gun, Educational and Recreational. 10 O.R. to U.K. for dispersal. 1 Officer to U.K. for med. to report to War Office for dispersal. Cricket Match.	
	12th		Picnic for A and B Companies, with Company Sports. Other 2 Companies usual Training.	
	13th		Usual Training.	

PAGE 2.

WAR DIARY
or
INTELLIGENCE SUMMARY.
(Erase heading not required.)

Army Form C. 2118.

Place	Date	Hour	Summary of Events and Information	Remarks and references to Appendices
STUMPF & DABRINGHAUSEN	14th		Usual Training. Concert by Battalion Party.	4/1/19
	15th		No Church Parades.	4/1/19
	16th		Training as usual. Short Range Work. 1 O.R. off strength (demob in U.K.) 1 Officer joined from 37th Bn. M.G.Corps.	4/1/19
	17th		Picnic for C and D Companies. Company Sports. Parades for other 2 Companies. No parades. "A" Company joined 2nd Sturm Inf. Bde at SOLINGEN. "B" Coy. remained in DABRINGHAUSEN. Orders received for move to BURG. Billetting party leaves for BURG. Day spent in packing up.	4/1/19
	18th		"A" Company under Orders of the 2nd Sturm Inf. Bde.	4/1/19
	19th		Left STUMPF at 09.00 hours and proceeded to SCHLOSS BURG. 1 Officer joined from 37th Bn. M.G.C	4/1/19
	20th		Cleaning equipment etc. No parades. "B" Company usual training whilst detached from Battalion.	4/1/19
	21st		Church Parades with Brigade Units, in Castle Courtyard BURG. Vol Services for R.C. and Pres.	4/1/19
	22nd		64 O.R. posted from 37th Bn. M.G.Corps. 5 Officers from 37th Bn. M.G.Corps. Preparing to move forward in event of Peace Terms not being signed. No parades.	4/1/19
	23rd		1 Officer for dispersal. No parades. Stand to for move.	4/1/19
	24th		7 O... Posted from 37th Bn. M.G.Corps and 1 Officers joined.	4/1/19
	25th		1 Officer joined from 37th Bn. M.G.Corps. Cleaning equipment limbers etc., Company full marching order inspection.	4/1/19
	26th		Time spent as per previous day. Inspection Parades under Company arrangements.	4/1/19
	27th		Parades under Company arrangements.	4/1/19
	28th		Parades under Company arrangements.	4/1/19
	29th		Church parades as per 21st inst.	4/1/19
	30th		Left BURG for STUMPF, and Dabringhausen.	4/1/19

CAPT. & ADJT.
29th BN. M. G. CORPS.

29th Battalion M.G. Corps

Army Form C. 2118.

WAR DIARY
or
INTELLIGENCE SUMMARY
(Erase heading not required.)

JULY 1919.

Place	Date	Hour	Summary of Events and Information	Remarks and references to Appendices
STUMPF & DABRINGHAUSEN	July 1st		General cleaning etc. on return from BURG & former billets at STUMPF & DABRINGHAUSEN.	M
	2nd		"A" & "B" Coys on short M.G. Rang. "C" & "D" Coys on musketry long Range. Officers taking M.G. Course in Batt "C" & "D" Coys Revolver practice. 1 O.R. struck off strength.	M
	3rd		"C" & "D" Coys on short Rang. "A" & "B" Coys musketry long Range. Revolver practice for "A" & "B" Coys.	M
	4th		GENERAL HOLIDAY. 5 O.R's to U.K. for disposal.	M
	5th		"A" & "B" Coys on short Rang. "C" & "D" Coys musketry long Rang. Revolver Practice for "C" & "D" Coys. 1 Officer in UK to attend Course at DABRINGHAUSEN.	M
	6th		CHURCH PARADES. "A" & "B" Coys in Church @ DABRINGHAUSEN. "C" & "D" Coys in STUMPF. Voluntary Holy Communion Evening Service.	M
	7th		As per 3rd inst. One officer struck off strength.	M
	8th		As per 5th inst. One officer to U.K. for Repatriation.	M
	9th		As per 3rd inst. Battn Cricket Match with 1/5 W. Yorks.	M
	10th		As per 5th inst.	M
	11th		As per 3rd inst.	M
	12th		As per 5th inst. One Officer struck off strength. Bn drafted with 1/5 Bde R.H.A.	M
	13th		CHURCH PARADES. "A" & "B" Coys at Church @ DABRINGHAUSEN. "C" & "D" Coys in STUMPF. Voluntary Holy Communion Evening Service.	M
	14th		Training as per 3rd inst. Battn cricket match with 2/4 Hampshire Regt. "London Div: M.T. Coy."	M
	15th		" " as per 5th inst. " "	M

29th Battalion M.G.C. Corps

Army Form C. 2118.

WAR DIARY
or
INTELLIGENCE SUMMARY
(Erase heading not required.)

JULY 1919

Place	Date	Hour	Summary of Events and Information	Remarks and references to Appendices
STUMPF & DABRINGHAUSEN	July 1st		General cleaning Etc. on return from BURG to former Billets at STUMPF & DABRINGHAUSEN.	M
	2nd		A + B Coys on short M.G. Rnges. C + D Coys musketry Long Range. Officers taking Miles Course. Batt. C + D Coys Revolver practice. 1 O.R. struck off strength.	M
	3rd		C + D Coys on Short Range. A + B musketry Long Range. Revolver Practice for A + B Coys.	M
	4th		GENERAL HOLIDAY. 5 O.R's to U.K. for dispersal.	M
	5th		A + B Coys Short Range. C + D Coys musketry Long Range. Revolver Practice for C + D Coys. 1 Officer to UK. for Clermont.	M
	6th		CHURCH PARADES A + B Coys in Church @ DABRINGHAUSEN C + D in STUMPF. Voluntary Holy Communion — Evening Service @ Recreation Room.	M
	7th		As per 3rd inst. One Officer struck off strength.	M
	8th		As per 5th inst. One Officer to UK. for Repatriation.	M
	9th		As per 3rd inst. Batt. Cricket Match with 1/5 W. Yorks	M
	10th		As per 5th inst.	M
	11th		As per 3rd inst.	M
	12th		As per 5th inst. One Officer struck off strength. BN Cricket match with 1/5 Bde R.G.A.	M
	13th		CHURCH PARADES. A + B Coys @ the Church @ DABRINGHAUSEN. C + D Coys in Recreation Room @ STUMPF. Voluntary Holy Communion. Evening Service.	M
	14th		Training as per 3rd inst. Batt. Cricket match with 2/4th Hampshire Regt.	M
	15th		" as per 5th inst. " " " "London Div. M.T. Coy"	M

WAR DIARY or INTELLIGENCE SUMMARY

Army Form C. 2118.

29th Batt M.G. Corps

Place	Date	Hour	Summary of Events and Information	Remarks and references to Appendices
STUMPF & DABRINGHAUSEN	July 16		Battalion Sports. One O.R. to U.K. (re-inlisted)	M
	17		Training as per 3rd inst. One O.R. struck off strength	M
	18		as per 5th inst. Lecture by Commander Repeated	M
	19		Range Practice for A & B Coys. Rewriter machine (Corps) boys NCO's Arms drill etc under R.S.M. 1 O.R. taken on strength	M
	20		CHURCH PARADES. A & B Coys in Church at DABRINGHAUSEN. C & D at Recreation Room STUMPF. Voluntary Holy Communion & Evening Service were held	M
	21st		Range Practice for C & D Coys. A & B Coys Revolver practice held under C.S.M. NCO's under R.S.M. One OR to U.K. for disposal	M
	22nd		Range Practice for A & B Coys C & D mg training still under C.S.M. NCO's under R.S.M. One Officer to U.K. for disposal	M
	23rd		Range Practice for C & D Coys. A & B mg Twenty ranks under C.S.M. NCOs under R.S.M. B.M Cricket match with 11th Hamps.td	M
	24th		Training as per 22nd inst. Inspection of Transport vehicles by Divisional Commander & Hotel Shoot. One OR taken on strength	M
	25		Training as per 23rd Bn cricket match with 24th Hants Regt.	M
	26		as per 22nd	M
	27		CHURCH PARADES. One Officer joined from 37th Bn M.G.C. A & B Coys in Church in DABRINGHAUSEN C&D in Recreation Room at STUMPF. Voluntary Holy Communion & Evening Service	M
	28		Training as per 23rd inst. One M.O. to U.K. for disposal. Cricket match	M
	29		as per 22nd. Western Divs Orchestral performance at DABRINGHAUSEN	M
	30		as per 23rd inst. Cricket match against 1/5 West Yorks at STUMPF	M
	31		as per 22nd. 2 OR to U.K. for disposal 1 OR taken on strength	M

M.R. Trethewaycroft
CAPT & ADJT
29th Bn M.G. Corps

29th Batt/n M.G. Corps

Army Form C. 2118.

WAR DIARY
or
INTELLIGENCE SUMMARY.
(Erase heading not required.)

Place	Date	Hour	Summary of Events and Information	Remarks and references to Appendices
STUMPF & DABRINGHAUSEN	July 16th		Battalion Sports. One O.R. to U.K. (re-enlisted)	M
	17th		Training as per 3rd inst. One O.R. struck off strength.	M
	18th		do. per 5th inst. Lecture by Command Paymaster.	M
	19th		Range Practice for A & B Coys. Revolver practice (C & D) Coys N.C.O.s Arms drill etc. when P.B.M. 1 O.R. taken on strength.	M
	20th		CHURCH PARADES. A & B Coys in Church at DABRINGHAUSEN. C & D at Recreation Room at STUMPF. Voluntary Holy Communion & Evening Service were held.	M
	21st		Range Practice for C & D Coys: A & B Coys. Revolver practice. Drill under Coys. Cmdrs. N.C.O.s under R.S.M. One O.R. to U.K. for Disposal.	M
	22nd		Range practice at B Coys C & D M.G. Training & Rifle under Coys. Cmdrs. One Officer to U.K. for dispersal.	M
	23rd		Range practice for C & D Coys. A & B Coys M.G. training with Coys. Cmdrs. N.C.O.s under R.S.M. Bn. Cricket match.	M
	24th		Training as per 22 inst. Inspection of transport vehicles by Divisional Commander for Horse Show. One O.R. taken on strength.	M
	25th		Training as per 23rd. Bn. Cricket match with 24th Hants. Regt.	M
	26th		as per 22nd. One Officer joined from 31st Bn M.G.C.	M
	27th		CHURCH PARADES. A & B Coys in Church at DABRINGHAUSEN. C & D in Recreation Room at STUMPF. Voluntary Holy Communion & Evening Service.	M
	28th		Training as per 23rd inst. One W.O. to U.K. for dispersal. Cricket match.	M
	29th		do. per 22nd. Western Div: Orchestral performance at DABRINGHAUSEN.	M
	30th		as per 23rd inst. Cricket match against 15th West Yorks at STUMPF.	M
	31st		as per 22nd. 2 O.R. to U.K. for Disposal. 1 O.R. taken on strength.	M

W.K. Shakyanturrah Capt. & Adjt.
1st 38th Bn. M.G. Corps.

Army Form C. 2118.

WAR DIARY
or
INTELLIGENCE SUMMARY
(Erase heading not required.)

AUGUST.

Instructions regarding War Diaries and Intelligence Summaries are contained in F. S. Regs., Part II. and the Staff Manual respectively. Title pages will be prepared in manuscript.

Place	Date	Hour	Summary of Events and Information	Remarks and references to Appendices
DABRINGHAUSEN & STUMPF.	1st	09.00 hrs to 13.00 hrs	Concert at Dabringhausen. Usual Educational Recreational and Machine Gun Training.	
	2nd	do.	Usual Training. 3men to U.K. for dispersal. Cricket Match.	
	3rd		Church Services at Dabringhausen and Stumpf.	
	4th		General Holiday.	
	5th	09.00 hrs to 13.00 hrs	1 Officer str. off strength sick to U.K. Usual Training. Cricket Match V 420th. Siege Batty. at Stumpf. Cricket Match with II Corps H.Q. at Leverkusen. Lena Ashwell Concert Party at Dabringhausen.	
	6th		do.	
	7th		do.	
	8th		do.	
	9th		do.	
	10th		Usual Church Services at Dabringhausen and Stumpf. 4 men for dispersal to U.K.	
	11th		Usual Training.	
	12th		do.	
	13th		do.	
	14th		Cricket Match V Xth Corps H.Q.	
	15th		1 O.R. to U.K. for dsipersal.	
	16th		MAXIMS Concert Party at Dabringhausen.	

Army Form C. 2118.

WAR DIARY
or
INTELLIGENCE SUMMARY.
(Erase heading not required.)

Instructions regarding War Diaries and Intelligence Summaries are contained in F. S. Regs., Part II. and the Staff Manual respectively. Title pages will be prepared in manuscript.

2. August.

Place	Date	Hour	Summary of Events and Information	Remarks and references to Appendices
	17th		Usual Church Services.	
	18th		Educational Machine Gun, and Recreational Training. Army Horse Show.	
	19th		do. 1 Officer to U.K. dispersal.	
	20th		do.	
	21st		do.	
	22nd		do. 4 men to U.K. for dispersal.	
	23rd		do. 2 men to U.K. for dispersal.	
	24th		Usual Church Services.	
	25th		Usual Training. 3 men to U.K. for dispersal	
	26th		do. 2 do. PEDLARS Concert Party at Dabringhausen.	
	27th		do. Cricket Match V R.A.O.C. Cologne. 2 Officers for dispersal to U.K.	
	28th		do. 5 men for dispersal to U.K.	
	29th		do. Cricket Match V 41st M.G.Bn. 3 O.R. to U.K. for dispersal.	
	30th		do. 4 men to U.K. for dispersal. MAXIMS Concert Party at Dabringhausen.	

CAPT. & ADJT,
29th BN. M. G. CORPS.

Army Form C. 2118.

WAR DIARY
or
INTELLIGENCE SUMMARY.
(Erase heading not required.)

Instructions regarding War Diaries and Intelligence Summaries are contained in F. S. Regs., Part II. and the Staff Manual respectively. Title pages will be prepared in manuscript.

Place	Date	Hour	Summary of Events and Information	Remarks and references to Appendices
Stumpf, Germany,	1/9/19		Parades 09.00 hours to 12.00 hours. 5 Officers to U.K. for dispersal.	
"	2/9/19.		Usual Parades. 09.00 hours - 12.00 hrs. Cricket match in the afternoon.	
"	3/9/19.		Usual Parades. Gun Drill, Stoppages etc.	
"	4/9/19.		Cricket Match, Semi-final of the Cologne Post Cup Competition, Versus 17th LANCERS, at 10.30 hrs.	
"	5/9/19.		Parades as usual. from 09.00 hours to 12.00 hrs (Gun drill, arms drill, etc).	
"	6/9/19		Parades as usual. 1 Officer and 15 Other ranks to U.K. for dispersal.	
"	7/9/19.		Usual Weekly Church Parades. 7 Other ranks to U.K. for dispersal. (5)	
"	8/9/19.		Usual Parades.09.00hrs.- 12.00 hrs. 9 other ranks to U.K. for dispersal. 1 Officer 43 O.R's to Army Rifle Meeting at DROVE.	
"	9/9/19.		Usual Parades 09.00hrs.- 12.00 hrs. 10 other ranks to U.K. for dispersal. 1 O.R. joined from BASE.	
"	10/9/19.		" " " 9 other ranks to U.K. for dispersal. 10 O.R.s received 2nd.Class Cert	
"	11/9/19.		26 O.R's receive 3rd.Class Cert. 7 other ranks to U.K. for dispersal.	
"	12/9/19.		Usual parades 09.00 hrs.-12.00 hrs. 3 officers and 10 O.R's to U.K. for dispersal.	
"	13/9/19.		Full Marching Order Inspection by the Commanding Officer. 9 Officers and 3 O.R's to U.K. for dispersal. Concert at 18.00 hrs. by the PRONGS CONCERT PARTY.	
"	14/9/19.		Usual SUNDAY CHURCH PARADES.	
"	15/9/19.		Usual parades from 09.00 hrs.-12.00 hrs. 9 Officers to U.K. for dispersal.	
"	16/9/19.		Usual parades.(Gun drill, etc). 5 O.R's to U.K. for dispersal. 5 Officers and 43 O.R's returned from Army Rifle Meeting, Drove.	
"	17/9/19.		Usual parades. 30 Other ranks to U.K. for dispersal.	
"	18/9/19		Rhine Army Boxing Championships. 20 Other ranks to U.K. for dispersal.	
"	19/9/19.		25 other ranks to U.K. for dispersal. 4 O.R's evacuated sick to U.K. and struck off strength.	
"	20/9/19.		Usual parades. 20 O.R's to U.K. for dispersal. Collection for British National Memorial at Ypres.21 O.R's to U.K. for dispersal.	
"	21/9/19.		Usual CHURCH PARADES.(Collection for British National Memorial at Ypres.21 O.R's to U.K. for dispersal.	
"	22/9/19.		70 other ranks to U.K. for dispersal.2 I O.R. undergoing detention transferred to Wandsworth Prison and	
"	23/9/19.		75 " " " " " " 4 officers to Con.Camp for conducting and is struck off strength.	
"	24/9/19.		Usual parades.	

Army Form C. 2118.

WAR DIARY
or
INTELLIGENCE SUMMARY.

(Erase heading not required.)

Instructions regarding War Diaries and Intelligence Summaries are contained in F. S. Regs., Part II. and the Staff Manual respectively. Title pages will be prepared in manuscript.

Place	Date	Hour	Summary of Events and Information	Remarks and references to Appendices
Stumpf, Germany.	25/9/19.		120 Other ranks to U.K. for dispersal.	
"	26/9/19.		20 Other ranks to U.K. for dispersal.	
"	27/9/19.		3 Other ranks rejoined from Course at Cologne, and 5 from leave to U.K. Leave and demobilisation can cell - ed owing to strike. 2 O.R's rejd. from Con.Camp. 1 other rank struck off strength on evacuation to U.K.	
"	28/9/19.		Usual SUNDAY CHURCH PARADES. 1 other rank rejoined from Concentration Camp.	
"	29/9/19.		Usual 09.00 hrs. inspection parade. 18 other ranks rejoined from Concentration Camp.	
"	30/9/19.		" " "	

W. Wilson Christ
CAPT. & ADJT.
29th BN. M. G. CORPS

Army Form C. 2118.

WAR DIARY
or
INTELLIGENCE SUMMARY.
(Erase heading not required.)

Instructions regarding War Diaries and Intelligence Summaries are contained in F.S. Regs., Part II. and the Staff Manual respectively. Title pages will be prepared in manuscript.

Place	Date	Hour	Summary of Events and Information	Remarks and references to Appendices
STUMPF nr COLOGNE.	1/10/19.			
	2/10/19.			
	3/10/19.		London Divisional Mule Gymkehana at Westhoven, Cologne.	
	4/10/19.		Usual Church Parades. 2 N.C.O.s Joined from Machine Gun School. Clocks put back one hour on railways only.	
	5/10/19.			
	6/10/19.			
	7/10/19.		One man struck off strength. To 3rd.Bettn. One man to course at 18th.M.V.S.	
	8/10/19.		One Officer and 22 O.R.s to U.K. for dispersal on 10th.	
	9/10/19.			
	10/10/19.		Two Officers to U.K. for dispersal.	
	11/10/19.			
	12/10/19.		Church Parades as usual. Winter Time taken into force in British Occupied Area.	
	13/10/19.		18 O.R.s to U.K. for dispersal.	
	14/10/19.		35 O.R.s to U.K. for dispersal.	
	15/10/19.			
	16/10/19.		7 O.R.s to U.K. for dispersal.	
	17/10/19.		One O.R. struck off strength and taken on strength of B.T.in E.& F. Major Reid-sptd 2nd.in Command of Battn.	
	18/10/19.		2 men successful at 2nd Class Army Cert Exam. 29/8/19.	
	19/10/19.		1 O/R. transferred to Southern Div.H.Q.Goy.	
	20/10/19.		10 passed Third Class Army Cert.Exam.	
	21/10/19.		6 O.R.s to U.K. for dispersal.	
	22/10/19.		2 Officers returned from Concentration Camp, Cologne (From conducting duty.)	
	23/10/19.		2 O.Rs to U.K. for dispersal.	
	24/10/19.		2 " " on re-enlistment furlough.	
	25/10/19.		5 Officers struck off strength. Authy.Rhine Army No.4 912/172(OI)	
	26/10/19.			
	27/10/19.		260 O.R.s on strength from 2nd.Bn & M.G.School.1officer fr	
	28/10/19.		5 O.R.s to U.K. for dispersal	

Army Form C. 2118.

WAR DIARY
or
INTELLIGENCE SUMMARY.
(Erase heading not required.)

Place	Date	Hour	Summary of Events and Information	Remarks and references to Appendices
STUMPF COLOGNE	29/10/19.		105 O.R.s on strength from 3rd.Bn.M.G.C. 2 Officers to U.K for dispersal.	
	30/10/19.		1 Officer to U.K. for dispersal.	
	31/10/19.		2 O.R.s to U.K. for dispersal. 1 O.R. evacuated to Hospital in U.K.	

A.P.Atkinson Brunt
CAPT. & ADJT.
29th BN. M. G. CORPS.

www.ingramcontent.com/pod-product-compliance
Lightning Source LLC
Chambersburg PA
CBHW080855230426
43662CB00013B/2111